P9-CLG-374

SMILING BEARS

A Zookeeper Explores the Behavior
and Emotional Life of Bears

ELSE POULSEN

Foreword by Stephen Herrero

GREYSTONE BOOKS

D&M PUBLISHERS INC.

VANCOUVER/TORONTO/BERKELEY

Copyright © 2009 by Else Poulsen

09 10 11 12 13   5 4 3 2 1

All rights reserved. No part of this book may be reproduced,
stored in a retrieval system, or transmitted, in any form or by any means,
without the prior written consent of the publisher or a license from
The Canadian Copyright Licensing Agency (Access Copyright). For a copyright
license, visit www.accesscopyright.ca or call toll free to 1-800-893-5777.

Greystone Books
A division of D&M Publishers Inc.
2323 Quebec Street, Suite 201
Vancouver, BC Canada V5T 4S7
www.greystonebooks.com

Library and Archives Canada Cataloguing in Publication
Poulsen, Else M. B
Smiling bears : a zookeeper explores the behavior and
emotional life of bears / Else Poulsen.

Includes index.
ISBN 978-1-55365-387-5

1. Poulsen, Else M. B. 2. Bears—Behavior. 3. Human-animal relationships. I. Title.

QL737.C27P685 2009   599.78   C2008-907846-2

Editing by Nancy Flight
Copy editing by Eve Rickert
Jacket design by Jessica Sullivan and Naomi McDougall
Text design by Ingrid Paulson
Jacket photograph by David Tipling/Getty Images

Printed and bound in Canada by Friesens
Printed on acid-free paper that is forest friendly (100% post-consumer
recycled paper) and has been processed chlorine free.

Distributed in the U.S. by Publishers Group West

We gratefully acknowledge the financial support of the Canada Council for the Arts,
the British Columbia Arts Council, the Province of British Columbia through the
Book Publishing Tax Credit, and the Government of Canada through the Book
Publishing Industry Development Program (BPIDP) for our publishing activities.

"Every form of nature has its own beauty."
RIGMOR ELISABETH BOGH POULSEN

"The more I get to know people, the better I
like animals!"   REV. OLAF POULSEN

To my nieces, the next generation—Kristen
and Rebecca Erin
    To my parents, Rigmor and Olaf; my
brother, Olaf, and my sister-in-law, Valerie;
and to my sister, Ellen, and my brother-in-
law, Robert

CONTENTS

FOREWORD

IN 1968 AND 1969, I got to know Jayne, Hazel, and their six cubs. They and thirty-four other American black bears whom I could identify regularly fed on people's stale bread, discarded hotdogs, and other leftovers at the Jasper town dump in Jasper National Park, Canada. I came to know each of these forty-two bears as an individual with distinct characteristics just like a person. Jayne appeared to be an experienced mother bear, with an unusually large family of four cubs. When she wanted to feed in a given spot, she could displace all the other bears including much larger male bears like Scarface. Jayne required her cubs to toe the line and follow wherever she went. If a cub got left behind, that seemed to be *his* problem, and in fact, in late fall, Jayne lost one cub.

Hazel appeared to be a young mother learning how to respond to two mile-a-minute, active cubs. She and her cubs often ran away and climbed a tree when other bears approached, compromising their opportunities to feed. At the conclusion of my research in Jasper, I felt I had been introduced to the complex nature of bear behavior and sociality. I knew bears were fascinating creatures. I wanted to learn more.

Additional understanding has come from people who have spent years getting to know individual bears and learning from their behavior. Terry DeBruyn's book *Walking with Bears*, Benjamin Kilham's *Among the Bears*, and Charlie Russell's *Grizzly Heart* have provided fascinating information about the nature and behavior of individual bears. Each book was based on years of observation and "living with" individual bears in their natural habitat. To this list of books that give insight into bears' heads, hearts, mouths, and stomachs must be added Else Poulsen's *Smiling Bears*. This is a book that had to be written, because Poulsen has such a burning passion for bears and their well-being. Over decades, she has made unique observations about the nature of individual bears and bear social groups. No one has ever before presented information about bears at this level of detail. As a bonus, the book presents well-written vignettes about first-hand experiences that Poulsen has had with individual bears.

Poulsen is an animal psychologist, zookeeper, animal trainer, and huge-hearted person with a passion for helping bears in captivity live better lives. She does this by trying to answer two basic questions for each bear: *Who are you?* and *What can I do for you?* She seeks answers by trying to develop a positive relationship with each bear to help shape his behavior toward a better life in captivity. To survive and be healthy enough to inspire admiration and conservation in viewers, a captive bear must adjust to his new environment. And often the bear must live in the same enclosure as other bears.

Imagine being responsible for bringing together eight polar bears, one of which was rescued from a severely abusive circus show, without ending up with a bunch of stressed and injured bears. Poulsen approached this challenge by first getting to know each bear and assessing her individual social needs and graces. Bärle was a small, hesitant nineteen-year-old female who had spent seventeen years in a cage where she could barely turn around. She was FedExed to her new home at the Detroit Zoo's new Arctic Ring of Life exhibit. Poulsen was part of a team that created a positive, enriched environment for these bears. The hope was to encourage each bear to express his or her basic genetic makeup and to eradicate aberrant behaviors. For the bears, there were treats to discover, a large tank to swim in, and seals, a polar bear's primary prey in nature, to watch. Rehabilitation of these bears began simply. For perhaps the first time, Bärle experienced clean straw bedding. Her reactions show her pleasure and Poulsen's sensitivity.

She locked in on the three-foot-high pile of fluffed straw so fresh you could smell it. Like a slow missile, Bärle headed right for it. She sniffed it, mouthed it, touched it with her paw. *Has she ever had so much clean straw all to herself before?* I wondered. Cautiously she stepped into it with one paw, then the other. Picking up speed, she crouched down on her belly, pushed her front legs behind her, and moved through the pile on her chest, pushing with her upright back legs. She flopped sideways into the pile and rolled onto her back, feet in the air, rubbing, gyrating, a smile on her face, saliva running from her nose and mouth. She seemed to be experiencing pure pleasure.

Bärle was a shy and hesitant bear whose introduction to each of the other polar bears had to be carefully designed to avoid trauma. Bärle proved to be her own salvation. Once comfortable with herself, she was able to manage each of the other bears' idiosyncrasies by reciprocating on his or her terms. Vilma, for example, was a wild child. Bärle figured out that Vilma wanted to play, especially in the water, so Bärle joined in and developed a lasting, positive relationship with Vilma.

An understanding of the potential social complexity of bears is something that is obtained only through patience, intimate association, and careful observation. These are the hallmarks of Poulsen's book.

I hate seeing large carnivores, like bears, enclosed, pacing back and forth, wheeling at each turn, along a fixed path. For me, this represents a captive environment that fails to meet the basic needs of the bear or other animal who lives there. Far from inspiring people, such a sight horrifies many, creating an image of an animal in an insane asylum. Poulsen has had to address pacing many times and has either solved it or at least temporarily alleviated it. She begins by helping to create an external environment for the bear that is interesting to explore, often one full of hidden treats to discover. For some bears, this is enough. But others' brains have become hardwired for pacing.

To address severe pacing, Poulsen proved herself to be as creative a problem solver as the bears whose environments she enriched. She observed that pacing in bears was similar to obsessive-compulsive disorder, an affective disorder in humans. Poulsen connected with a neuroscientist, and together they tested the theory of an affective disorder in Snowball, an old female polar bear with a pacing problem. They stopped her pacing by giving her the drug Prozac. This achievement brought joy for Poulsen, but when the drug treatment was stopped, the pacing soon returned. Apparently, such drug treatment can play a role in addressing pacing, but since it does not necessarily cure it, the best approach is to prevent the initiation of pacing by providing a healthy environment in the first place.

Smiling Bears contains a wealth of useful information for professional managers of bears. In captivity, bears' behavior is usually molded into something that works both for the animals, given their genetic nature, and for their keepers. For example, bears can be trained to present their heads to receive eye drops. Training consists of giving bears little treats as they get closer and closer to doing what is needed. With treats such as grapes, a skilled keeper like Poulsen can train a bear to do many things. Her experience helps wildlife managers understand why a few instances of eating people's food or garbage can create a lifelong problem that is difficult to stop. Bears are hugely motivated to eat and get fat.

Smiling Bears also speaks to biologists who may have spent much of their professional careers studying bear populations, usually to derive population estimates so as to be better able to conserve bears. Some bear biologists have captured and marked hundreds of bears without ever knowing any one as an individual. An extreme stereotyping can result in which bears are seen as being part of a class, such as adult males, with little or no thought given to bears as individuals. Everyone who associates with bears can learn much from this book about the animals' varied personalities and abilities.

Poulsen's writing will expand every reader's understanding and appreciation of bears. Through her anecdotes and evidence you will discover that bears plan how to manipulate other bears and even their keepers. You will find out that bears do smile, and when and why. You might not agree with all of Poulsen's interpretation of bear behavior, but I guarantee that she will make you think. Some will say the book is too anthropomorphizing—ascribing human thoughts, plans, and feelings to bears. Read *Smiling Bears* and judge for yourself. You will probably also conclude, as I have, that locking an animal as complex as a bear into a sterile captive environment is unethical and unacceptable.

By writing *Smiling Bears*, Poulsen has answered her own second question: *What can I do for you?* This book will contribute immensely to a more accurate, much more broad-based understanding of the nature of bears. This is Poulsen's contribution to bears and to the people who are drawn to them.

Stephen Herrero, PhD
Professor Emeritus of Environmental Science,
University of Calgary, Alberta

ACKNOWLEDGMENTS

HUMANS ARE NOT independent creatures like bears. We depend on each other and can take credit for very little alone. An extreme thank you to all of these friends who have taught me much, have been such an inspiration, and most importantly have taken time out of their busy lives to help bears and bear people:

Robyn Appleton, Bruce Armon, Ophelia Barringer, Christine Bartos, John Beecham, Mark Bekoff, Sandy Black, Donald N. Blakeley, Diane Bradley, Carol Bresnay, Karen Brocklehurst, Robert and Carolyn Buchanan, the Calgary Zoo Docents, the Calgary Zoo Construction Crew, Grace Cameron, Scott Carter, Brenda and Brian Dalrymple, Terry Debruyn, Linda Denomme, the Detroit Zoo Docents and Volunteers, Pat Dodge, Tami and John Doran, Bill Dubreuil, Jody Edwards, Brenda Eeglon, Diane Farrell, Kathy Jo Ferguson, Nancy Flight, Lydia Fogal, Tina Gagnon, Jeff Gerecke, Tony Grant, Gina Greco, Valerie Hare, Gail Hedberg, Stephen Herrero, Ginny Honeyman, Patricia Mills

Janeway, Bligh Jenkins, Christin Jones, Else Bogh Juhl, Ron Kagan, Peter Karsten, Benjamin Kilham, Sue Kingsepp, Bob Klassen, Lydia Kolter, Caroline Kudwa, Ellen Kulie, Rob Laidlaw, Pierre Lebrun and Calgary Zoo Security, Brenda Lefevre, Jai Longhurst, Ron Manseau, Jeffrey Moussaieff Masson, Melanie McAuley, Jan and Joe McCarthy, Terry McDonald, Carrie McIntyre, Betsie Meister, Larry Miller, Alice Ng, Amy Ng, Linda Opipari, Catharine Page, Bob Peel, Carol Petrone, Jennifer Pouliot, Peggy Powers, Jason Pratte, Jim Price, Pam Pritchard, Dave, Carol, Ryan and Evan Cheung Quan, Judith Rapoport, Richard Rausch, Harry Reynolds, Eve Rickert, Jill Robinson, Amy Rose, Katherine Roth, Tom Roy, Rob Sanders, Kasey and Callen Schoff, Julie Seguin, Michelle Seldon, JoAnne Simerson, Evelyn Smith, Rebecca Snyder, Cedric Stapleton, Ian Stirling, Kevin Strange, Greg Tarry, Cam Teskey, Audrey Tournay, Amy Vaerewyck, Pamela Valentine, Sue and Les Vestre, Dawn Vien, Shawna Wilkinson, Judy Willard, Elaine Willms, Bob Wojtowicz, Karen Worley, Alexander Worobey, Matt Wort, and Jackson Zee.

WHO ARE YOU AND WHAT CAN I DO FOR YOU?

MY PARENTS REMEMBER the first bear I ever saw. It was 1958, and I was three. We were on our annual August trek from Baltimore to the West Coast and back again in the family station wagon. On the outgoing trip, we stopped by a river in Yellowstone National Park for a break. My parents used a fallen tree trunk as a picnic table, and my older brother and I ran around blowing off steam after having been confined to the car much of the morning.

The riverbank was quiet and secluded. The only other human was a fisherman, who stood very still fishing downstream, waiting patiently for a bite. As we ate, I'm told, a black bear came out of the woods, crossed the road, and ambled down to the river's edge. Hanging her head and peering intently into the lake, she stood motionless. Suddenly, she slammed her upper torso into the lake and came up, water streaming off her fur, with a large trout flopping in her mouth. Then she crossed the road and disappeared back into the trees with her catch. The fisherman continued to stand very still fishing downstream, waiting patiently for a bite, and we finished our picnic.

Bears and other wildlife were not an unusual sight on our many visits to America's national parks. As kids we were told that wild animals, particularly bears, needed room to be themselves. We obeyed the Do Not Feed the Bears signs, and my father would slowly navigate the station wagon through the human bear jams on the road without stopping. Even in my child's mind, I could appreciate my parents' good sense, since bears seemed big, powerful, and unpredictable. And humans who got out of their cars to hand-feed them cookies seemed like, well, *bear bait.*

My mother has since told me that in the 1950s and '60s people knew very little about bear behavior, and visitors to the parks were generally not afraid of bears. It seemed that if you left them alone, they would just mosey on their way, unless you fed them, which many did. My father and mother can both remember hearing a park naturalist say that feeding a bear a cookie or two would not hurt the bear, but that the bear would not understand when the bag was empty. The bear would become angry, assuming that you were withholding cookies, and would tackle you for more or go looking for other food in your car.

In July 1968, on another road trip across America, my father looked after my kid sister, Ellen, in the station wagon while my mother, my brother, and I hiked the Water Ouzel Trail off Going-to-the-Sun-Road in Glacier National Park, Montana. I was thirteen, and annoyingly, my brother, Olaf Johannes, was still three years older and caught on to everything before I did. He used this occasion to read aloud mock park literature about killer bears on this very trail, just to torment me. I was terrified!

My mother cheerily told me that we should just clap our hands and the bears would run away. I didn't believe a word of it; what self-respecting bear would run off just because a human clapped her hands? I knew my limitations as a thirteen-year-old human—why wouldn't the bear also understand that I was vulnerable and likely edible? And what bear wouldn't be annoyed that there were humans on his trail and try to chase them off? I would if I were a bear. The hike seemed long and arduous, and I couldn't wait for it to end.

Now I know that my mother was right. No bear would want to be around a loud brother terrorizing his sister, a loud sister protesting her brother's existence, and a noisy mother attempting to demonstrate the hand-clapping technique to her two unruly subadult cubs.

AFTER GRADUATING FROM university, I found work as a field biologist for an environmental consulting company in Calgary, Alberta. We did environmental impact assessments of proposed projects for energy companies in the oil patch, which often seemed like a contradiction in terms. Each project meant yet another piece of land restructured, used up and distorted, and more animal refugees created. The idea of land reclamation was new and developing. Our fieldwork took us mostly to the prairies, where the oil, sour gas, and coal were.

In my free time, I learned to hike and ski mountains. In the Rocky Mountains, I came to understand what rugged, remote wilderness truly was. And I fell in love. I fell in love with meeting the challenge of climbing to the summit, hearing the crunch of dry snow packing under your felt-lined boots as you walked, and standing on a mountain so quiet that you could hear snowflakes falling on your jacket and, in contrast, the booming echo of avalanches in the distance. I fell in love with seeing wolves in the valley below, finding cougar tracks in the mud, and discovering grizzly bears. I loved that grizzly bears lived there, that they raised their young there, that they found mates and food and solace there.

My brother and I went hiking again in Glacier National Park, this time as adults, in September 1998. We parked at the Logan Pass Visitor Information Center to walk the Hidden Lake Overlook trail. While I was waiting for my brother, who was still inside the center, I joined a small group of people outside the building who were watching an enormous, chestnut-colored male grizzly bear in the alpine meadow across the valley. He was busy grubbing for foods such as lily tubers and ground squirrels. He dug as he walked in a spiral, adding rings of tilled land to the circumference of the circle. I was mesmerized.

Olaf came out and wanted to speed-walk to Hidden Lake. I didn't want to leave the grizzly bear but reluctantly joined him. For a few minutes, I jogged behind my speed-walking brother, who was several hundred yards ahead of me on the trail. My heart decidedly wasn't in this. I pulled a u-turn and ran back to watch the bear. There were other groups on the trail to Hidden Lake, so I wasn't concerned about my brother hiking alone. The grizzly was still digging. He was built like a furry tank—massive, blocklike, and seemingly unstoppable—and yet, when he noticed something of interest, he gently sieved the soil from the plant with his claws and ate what he found. I was part of a small, privileged group of admirers, all standing very still, quietly awestruck. When my brother returned two hours later, the bear's crop circle was nearly a hundred feet in diameter.

In 1984, when oil prices fell and the bottom dropped out of the energy industry, my employer declared bankruptcy, and I was unemployed. I took what I thought would be a temporary position as a zookeeper at the Calgary Zoo just to ride out the economic storm. Instead, caring for animals became my life's work, which took me from Calgary to Detroit, Denmark, Indonesia, and Singapore. Being a zookeeper is not a job; it's a way of life. As a zookeeper, you are responsible for the complete well-being of the animals in your care. That means feeding and cleaning them, creating complex living environments, lobbying on their behalf to managers, and educating the public and often other zoo staff.

The 1980s were an exciting time to begin a career as a zookeeper. It was a time of upheaval for zoos as they and the public began to question the welfare of animals living in small, concrete, barred cages. It was no longer acceptable to see sensory-deprived bears pacing up and down in response to living in barren exhibits. At the same time, information about the animals' behavior was pouring out of the wilderness as technological advances in tool and clothing materials allowed biologists to do fieldwork in extreme environments. Progressive zoo professionals applied data from the wild to captive animals' living environments, and those animals responded by living mentally and physically healthy lives. This period of reformation continues today but is not without its bumps and detours along the way.

ANY ZOO REFLECTS its country's cultural beliefs about the true value of animals as well as that country's lifestyle and societal trends. North America—the Western world—is steeped in the fads and trends of urban life for the obvious reason that most of us live in large urban environments. Phrases like "street chic" and "metrosexual" seep into our language and color our human-centric perception of the world around us. Even progressive zoos, richly influenced by Western values, spend millions of dollars catering to this impatient, self-indulgent culture by building exhibits meant to totally immerse experience-hungry visitors in cement reproductions of nature, using live animals as props for the display. These zoos have detoured from their original objective: to provide animals with enclosed environments—homes—that they can healthfully live in. Bears in these mock-natural environments experience the cement as they always have, as cement. Unable to find a use for cement and the small exhibit space, they pace, as they always have.

Despite exhibitory fads meant to wring dollars out of donors and visitors, we are moving forward as a society and demanding better care of all the animals in our midst. Zoos, sanctuaries, and rehabilitation facilities are collaborating to maximize their conservation resources and to share husbandry techniques that benefit bears. For example, the Bear Care Group is a charitable organization based in North America whose sole purpose is to promote bear welfare and conservation by organizing international bear care conferences and workshops for captive-bear caregivers that focus exclusively on excellence in bear care.

It isn't realistic to think that there will ever be a time when bears will not be in captivity, as our population grows and humans move deeper and deeper into former wilderness areas and displace all forms of wildlife there. Wild bears end up being orphaned or injured and need rehabilitation. Although bear rehabilitation is not yet as common as it will become as the science behind it improves—many bears are sent directly to zoos and sanctuaries—some bears are rehabilitated and released back into the wild. Bears that cannot be released are either euthanized for compassionate reasons (if they have permanent, life-threatening conditions) or sent to sanctuaries or zoos if their disabilities allow them to live otherwise healthy lives.

As I gained experience with bears, I came to understand that no matter how large, natural, or complex, all captive environments are substandard, the standard being the wild. The wild offers bears opportunity—a chance to be self-sufficient, find food and a mate, raise young, develop, and be challenged. Essentially, zookeepers spend their time making up for what is missing in the environments of the animals in their care. I have approached every animal with the same two questions on my mind: *Who are you?* and *What can I do for you?* It is impossible to effectively care for a bear unless you can answer those two questions, and they have been the driving force of my work.

Like a human, a bear is the sum total of his genetic makeup, his experience, and his ability to adapt these to new circumstances. To find out who a bear is, I have had to study the research from the wild, dig up the bear's personal history, and, most important, develop a relationship with the animal to have some sense of his expectations. Like a human, every bear on Earth wants something—from his environment, his cohorts, and his caretakers, whether they are furry parents or zookeepers. A bear will not share his thoughts with you if he doesn't know you or if he knows you but doesn't trust you.

When I first began work as a zookeeper in the early 1980s, I was fortunate to learn from a few highly successful zookeepers who developed trusting relationships with their animals. The animals, since they trusted the keepers, would move easily from one enclosure to another or allow the zookeepers to come into their enclosure with them to clean and to place food, thus reducing the animals' and keepers' overall stress levels. We discussed the animals' ability to understand human behavior and to communicate with us and each other—privately, since those ideas (and the zookeepers) would have been publicly ridiculed by colleagues and managers. At that time, only apes were considered sentient beings, because they were most like us. But I understood early on that, to make a difference in the life of a bear, I had to develop a meaningful relationship—meaningful to the bear. Since no two bears are alike, making friends is different each time.

Misty, for example, was an adult polar bear rescued from the wild who lived for years at the Calgary Zoo with Snowball, a captive-born female polar bear. Misty was content to remain in the background and let Snowball do all the interacting with zookeepers. After Snowball died, Misty was alone for the first time in her life. A few days after Snowball's death, Misty surprised me by coming into the back dens while I was cleaning up the keeper areas. She just stood still and watched me. I was overjoyed but didn't make a big happy fuss, since it would likely have scared her off. Periodically I looked up from my work and spoke to her softly. She kept me company like this for weeks. Over time I was allowed to come close enough to the bars to treat her with grapes. These were the first steps on the path to communication between two friends.

In contrast, a leg-climbing, people-biting, angry little American black bear desperado named Miggy arrived motherless at the Detroit Zoo, where I was working at the time. She was eight months old and small for her age, and she was completely lost, aimless in her overzealous, pinball-like activity. I tried to calm her by entering her pen to offer foods, company, and gentle touching. Each time, she attacked me. Miggy needed a bear mom, and my behavior toward her was not giving the right cues or meeting her needs. Her small size suggested that she was developmentally behind. To assess this, I entered her pen and sat down on the ground. I slowly rocked back and forth while quietly humming, behavior I had observed in mother bears nursing their young. Bingo: Miggy immediately plunked herself into my lap. For lack of mother's milk, I fed her chopped apples. She responded with a soft, guttural neighing sound that contented bear cubs make.

Although I was a poor excuse for a bear mother, Miggy adapted out of need—her desire to survive. Many people ask me if captive bears are like wild bears. Yes, they are exactly the same animal, with a different set of skills.

You and I know how to stay alive in an urban community. As humans, we are genetically encoded to adapt to many environments when given proper teaching from more experienced humans. We know not to talk to strangers, not to cross on the red light, and not to leave the doors unlocked. Most of us are more or less successful and only occasionally make a life-threatening mistake. Some of us may have an additional set of survival skills, depending on our circumstances. We can live with a debilitating disease, be shot into space and live in a capsule, or survive summer camp. After summer camp, we are still the same people we were before summer camp, except now we know to write our name in our underwear, not to chew gum found under the bed, and to stay away from things that look like sticks but are, in fact, snakes.

But what if someone picked us up and dropped us off, with no warning and no luggage, in the Gobi desert to live for the rest of our lives? Just you and me, and sand everywhere, underfoot and in the air. Eye-stinging, nostril-burning, airborne sand on hot, dry winds. No energy bars, no water bottles, no tents made of space-age materials—just sand. We will either die or survive. Our survival depends entirely on our ability to adapt.

After walking for hours in the unchanging landscape, we see a ger tent belonging to a hospitable nomadic Mongolian family. We are grateful to be offered sour mare's milk, goat's curd, and flat bread. Tomorrow the family is moving north, toward water and low-lying shrubbery for their livestock. We are welcome to join them if we can help with the cashmere goat herding and shearing. You and I are still the same people that we were before we arrived in the Gobi desert, but now we herd goats for our survival.

As it is for us, so it is for bears; to adapt is to survive, and survival is everything. Each bear is an individual and survives differently from the next. Although I have known and continue to know many more bears, I chose to write about the bears who appear in this book because they illustrate how different bears are in their personality, intellect, fortitude, and emotions.

Chapter 1 is about bears as sentient beings and how we perceive them. Bears have always been who they are, but our understanding and study of their sentience is still in its infancy. The rest of the chapters are about the bears themselves and how they responded to whatever circumstances they were in. I have placed the stories in chronological order, but since bears are long-lived, and since I worked with more than one species of bear at a time, some of the time periods overlap. The epilogue presents the stories of some of the relentlessly dedicated people who rescue and conserve bears on our planet. Information about their organizations and other bear conservation groups is given in the appendix. It is my greatest hope that by reading this book you will come to know bears on a personal level and will be inspired to help the bears in your neighborhood, whether they are in a zoo, sanctuary, or rehabilitation facility or in the wild.

SMILING BEARS

CHAPTER 1

SMILING BEARS

Bears Do Things for Bear Reasons

TINY, A SMALL, adult female American black bear living at the Calgary Zoo, inched forward, one slow step at a time, head lowered, eyes focused, nose pointing toward a cache of peanuts already claimed by her sister. Ears, a rotund female—twice Tiny's size—looked sideways at her a couple of times and kept on eating. Tiny's nose doggedly came closer. When it was less than a foot from the pile, Ears exploded into jaw snapping, clacking her teeth together and huffing with quick expulsions of air from her mouth as she gave chase. Tiny raced around an island of thick conifers, staying just far enough ahead of Ears to be out of sight. On the third go-around, Tiny leapt off the radius path into a grassy opening and sat in broad view, watching Ears still chasing her in circles. Ears forged on in an angry heat until she noticed Tiny sitting in the open watching her. Ears slowed down, running off her speed until she came to a stop, then turned her rump toward Tiny. Head hanging and body slumped, she feigned interest in the dead twigs at her feet, sniffing and mouthing them with her lips. She stole several sideways glances at Tiny, who was still staring at her, smiling.

Bears are born with the mental and physical flexibility required to negotiate the environment in which they are meant to live. This is true for spiders, humans, rats—all animals. Bears have personalities, individual differences, that set the template for how they address life. This too is true for humans and rats, but spiders—well, maybe.[1] Humans have spent thousands of years trying to position ourselves at the top of a man-made creature hierarchy based on the frailties we perceive in other species. To this day, we have not been able to fully answer the question *What is it to be human?* without denigrating other species. As a result of our own species-identity crisis, we have lost touch with the living things around us. The twentieth-century dogma that we must not anthropomorphize, or attribute human characteristics like emotions to animals, has moved several generations of humans farther away from understanding the creatures we share the planet with.

The self-aggrandizing and widespread assumption that we humans have the full complement of all of the emotions possible to all animals on Earth—basically, that all the marbles belong to us—is not only unscientific but also childish. Do we know how it feels to sail on an updraft in the sky, to echolocate our dinner in the dark, or to see at lightning speed with a compound eye? Fortunately, human understanding is maturing, and we are learning that animals are emotional, thinking, and self-aware beings relative to the niche that they were born to occupy. Scientists have identified and are investigating biophilia; the idea suggests that we humans have an innate need to be with the living things around us.[2]

And we do, every day—we just don't always recognize it. Where do we go when we need a vacation? We migrate in flocks to beaches, mountains, and cottages in the woods. Why? For the same reason that our children are unabashedly thrilled with the accessible living things in their world, such as bugs, leaves, birds, and small rodents for pets. We are biophiliacs—not a pleasant-sounding word, which will likely have an image problem when it hits mainstream consciousness—and the living world appeals to us cognitively, emotionally, and physically.

When I was a zookeeper, my everyday experiences with animals left me wondering if the researchers who cling to the ideas that animals have no feelings, no problem-solving abilities, and no self-awareness had ever interacted with their family cat or dog. But thought evolves, and there is a fresh breeze blowing common sense into our thinking. Free-thinking ethologists recommend that we learn to apply our biophiliac abilities rather than denying them. Gordon Burghardt suggests that we use critical anthropomorphism to incorporate what we know about an animal's life history, adaptations, and behavior into our scientific deductions.[3] Marc Bekoff agrees and suggests that we adopt a biocentric anthropomorphic attitude, trying to see the animals' world from their perspective.[4]

I suggest that nature selects for cross-species communication and understanding. A deer that doesn't understand what two coyotes are doing when they follow him in tandem is a dead deer who doesn't live to breed another day! Scientists have observed badgers and coyotes going hunting together for squirrels, marmots, and prairie dogs.[5] To be effective, the badger and the coyote need to be able to communicate positions and intent with each other and understand each other's behavior. They must also have a working knowledge of their prey's behavior. To care for and to better the lives of the bears in my charge, I use a pragmatic, applied anthropomorphism to understand their needs, and I approach every bear with the same two questions on my mind: *Who are you?* and *What can I do for you?*

A bear has a reason for everything she does, and that reason is based on genetic heritage, internal or external cues, and personal history. In short, bears do things for bear reasons. Bears smile. It has been my experience that when a bear smiles she is expressing a sense of contentment. The reason for contentment may be something like finding a cache of thousands of fat, juicy moth larvae at the summit of the mountain, which may not be something that would make a human feel content. The bear hopes that the larvae will be there after she climbs all the way up the steep slope because the larvae were there last year and it was a feast. And yes, they are there again this year, gobs of them, and that could well be worth smiling about.

Smiling bears (both wild and captive) have been documented in hundreds of photographs, but the meaning of the smile and its relationship to feeling good about something is a topic that only those who have worked closely with bears can address. Jill Robinson, founder of Animals Asia and two Asian black bear sanctuaries, is one of those people. In her work to free and rehabilitate hundreds of bears from the horror of bear bile farms, she has observed broad smiles on the faces of recovering bears:

> The contrast between the depleted shells of animals newly arriving from the bile farms and the characters of the bears

today could not be more extreme. Initially and understandably, eyes burn with fear and loathing and mouths open and vocalize aggressively from animals unable to distinguish between members of a species now desperately trying to help them, and the same species responsible for their suffering on the farms. The gradual transition of their character and personality is remarkable. As they heal in roomy recovery cages, their eyes no longer convey hatred and distrust but gaze calmly at our staff, seemingly cognizant that they have nothing to fear. Finally released into dens and enclosures, the bears develop their personalities as profound and individual as any human. Lifelong friendships are formed, dizzy, hilarious interactions in what is supposed to be a solitary species. We have learned to be unconcerned with accusations of anthropomorphism from the scientific community as we watch these bears now smile radiantly in their pleasure and play—convinced that, one day, science will prove us right.

MORE OF ROBINSON's remarkable story rescuing China's bears is told in the epilogue.

It's impossible to fully interpret the behavior of another living thing. Your chances of accurate interpretation are better if you are of the same species, but even that doesn't guarantee understanding. Aren't there times when your neighbor's behavior is a complete mystery? Spending time with the individual helps to add information about what came before and after the behavioral scenario you are trying to decode. The first of the many times I witnessed the scenario between Tiny and Ears, my impression was that Tiny had baited Ears into a chase and then purposely sat by and watched as Ears embarrassed herself by chasing nothing around the island, behavior that made Tiny smile. But did the evidence support that conclusion?

Mulling it over, I wondered if this was play. The usual communication gestures that bears use to express playful intent, such as swinging their head from side to side a couple of times or using floppy, exaggerated body movements, were missing. My best clue in interpreting the seriousness of this event came from Patches, the third sister in the group, who galloped off when the row began.

The three bears had been orphaned as cubs in a forest fire in British Columbia and raised at the Calgary Zoo. Ears was the largest sister but was not a fast learner. She became aggressive when provoked, and Tiny frequently provoked her by lying in her day bed or by sitting and staring at her. These were bold moves for a small bear.

The second and third times I observed Tiny run Ears in circles, I was convinced that Tiny was purposely illustrating to Ears that Tiny could manipulate her, thus giving Ears a subordinate position. Tiny may simply have been smiling because she liked to control Ears, but the smile reinforced her status as number one. Patches didn't have Tiny's gall and stayed neutral. She waited until the others had chosen foods or nesting sites and settled for what was left, putting herself at the bottom of the hierarchy. With Tiny at the helm, there were constant arguments, unrest, and dissatisfaction in the group. I had to level the playing field.

Food was of prime importance to the bears. If every bear was successful in the competition for preferred foods, the stress levels would be negated or reduced. The animal care volunteers and I scattered a great variety of foods—apples, pears, melons, grapes, mealworms, raisins, nuts, willow branches—around the enclosure, betting that Tiny could not be everywhere at the same time and thus that Ears and Patches would have a shot at retrieving favorite treats without interference. It worked. Tiny had her choice of treats, but so did the other girls. Ears completely ignored Tiny's next baiting attempts, so Tiny went after Patches, who also stood her ground for the first time, staring firmly at Tiny while munching on a treat. Tiny's rule had been toppled. A more relaxed atmosphere ensued as Tiny gave up most of her intimidation tactics, but there was no Disney ending here.

Tiny still had some realistic concerns. At any given time, she was the smallest bear by at least sixty-five pounds. To meet her own needs in the face of her giant and mid-sized sisters, she had devised a strategy that was energy consuming for her and oppressive for others, but it worked. I took that away, and it made her uneasy. Several times Tiny came up to stare straight at me, her nose lowered, her mouth a thin, short slit—no smiles, no floppy playful moves, and no sniffy greetings. I felt blamed. And it *was* my fault. I made a point of monitoring Ears' and Patches' behavior to make certain that no new coups were brewing. None were. When food was scattered, it was easily accessible to everyone, and Ears and Patches—now self possessed— minded their own foraging business.

In this case, all of the information we needed to interpret behaviors and solve the problem were readily available, but that isn't always so. I worked with a twenty-three-year-old male polar bear named Nanuq at a small, remote facility. He had lived peaceably with two four-year-old sisters for a few months when his behavior radically changed. It was early spring, and Nanuq began to follow both females around the enclosure, courting them. After a few days, one female showed interest and they bred. The other sister did not cycle and continued to show him her pointy upper lip, huffing at him, sometimes cuffing him in the head and running away. Although Nanuq was persistent, he was never pushy. These behaviors were entirely expected and understood. When spring arrived in earnest, so did the nocturnal moose roadkill. We eviscerated and quartered the moose and placed sections of the meat in the exhibit as far apart as possible, giving each bear an opportunity for privacy when eating.

Nanuq became increasingly anxious, aggressively herded the females into the farthest northwest corner of the exhibit, and threatened them by jaw snapping, huffing, and chasing them when they attempted to escape his direction. Despite the huffy display, he didn't seem angry with them, just oddly busy, which is likely why the girls initially felt secure enough to separate and run circles around him. But Nanuq remained aggressive, and eventually the females grew fearful of him. One night he dragged each of the moose quarters back together into a great pile in the southeast end of the enclosure—no small task since each section easily weighed three hundred pounds. Most perplexing of all, he sprawled himself like a huge blanket on top of the pile, seeming to take ownership.

I have observed male bears give females gifts of food, sticks, and bedding during courtship and, on rare occasions, being overly aggressive, but I have never seen a male directly withhold food from females during breeding season. Nanuq eventually became so bossy that we had to separate him from the females to give them some peace. Then suddenly all the behaviors fell into place.

A security guard had observed an American black bear male wandering the perimeter of the facility fence each evening.

Talking to locals, I learned that the facility had been built in the black bear's territory, something this bear didn't easily let go of. He had come out of winter denning and smelled two female bears, one of whom was cycling, and a cache of fresh moose meat. Nanuq was under siege. He was responding to the threat of another male—even if the male was a smaller American black bear—as he herded *his* females to the northwest part of the enclosure, which was the farthest point from the spot where Nanuq could see the black bear standing on the outside of the perimeter fence, looking in. Then he dragged *his* moose meat into a single pile, where he could guard it and watch the black bear at the same time. Draping himself over the meat was the coup de grâce, meaning, mine! It was a wonderfully reasoned and executed plan to protect home and hearth.

Bears are governed strictly by their genetic sensibilities, and I have been bitten, huffed at, paw slammed, and stared at in disbelief or disappointment if I didn't get it right and do it the bear way. It has been my experience that, to male bears in particular, ownership matters. Regardless of how humans think the scenario should play out or think is best for the bear, nothing but resolution of the problem as the bear perceives it will settle the issue. And therein lies the challenge.

Petey was a fourteen-year-old, 450-pound male American black bear who paced all day for five months despite the best efforts of the Maryland Zoo staff to give him alternative things to do. It began when he was upgraded—by human standards—from his small enclosure to one that was twice as big and had a larger pool. The move was made to accommodate an elderly, 1,200-pound grizzly bear named Junior who needed a smaller, less-challenging enclosure because he was having trouble getting around. It seemed perfect; Junior got Petey's old enclosure, and Petey got a much larger, more challenging place to live. My colleague Christine Bartos, Petey's head zookeeper, called me to consult about the matter. Petey's pacing pattern focused on one site, where he could see the grizzly bear on *his land*. To my mind, it wasn't a coincidence that he chose to pace there. Another bear had taken over his home. Even if the interloper was an ambulatory-challenged ancient bear and even if it was a lesser-quality plot, Petey was under siege, and to intensify the frustration, Petey couldn't get there to defend what was his.

We developed a plan. Petey couldn't focus on his new digs as long as he had a constant visual reminder of his loss and his inability to deal with it. We blocked the view with a blind. This didn't mean that Petey would suddenly forget that he had lost property to another bear, but at least the issue was no longer staring him in the face. By blocking the view, we had turned his attention inward to his new home, which meant that his new home had better meet with his bear standards and maintain his interest, or he would continue to pace. The keepers immersed Petey in meaningful enrichment that included a digging bed, and he had bedding materials, scent trails and depots, natural foods such as fresh tree branches to strip, foods scattered throughout the enclosure, and puzzle feeders made from capped PVC pipe with holes to allow foods to drop out when manipulated. His new space was again doubled when he was given permanent access to the neighboring enclosure so that he could be reunited with his sister, from whom he had been separated for reproductive reasons years earlier. It worked. Although at first Petey frequently went back to check the blinded area, he did refocus his attention on his new property and stop pacing.

In the previous three vignettes, I had time to think and rethink, research, distill, and assess. But every day I had to solve on-the-spot problems based on my knowledge, experience, and my anthropomorphic gut.

Sissy was a twenty-seven-year-old female polar bear who lived at the Detroit Zoo. I came to check on her first thing one morning for a visit that would become one of the most poignant moments of personal communication I have had with a bear. The afternoon before, she had had several decaying molars removed in dental surgery. She had successfully come out from under the anesthetic and been given painkillers, antibiotics, and access to water. We left her in the evening, sleeping on the floor in one of the bedrooms in the polar bear building. It was now a little after seven AM, and I found Sissy lying on her sternum in the middle of the floor, facing the wall, her white fur covered in a gooey mix of saliva tinted with bloody pink blotches. There were also pools of goo on the floor. Her eyelids were drooping, and she looked tired from yesterday's ordeal. I decided to leave in case she wanted to continue sleeping, but she had heard me and got up. So I stayed and began speaking softly to her.

Sissy and I had been down this road before. The previous summer, she had developed a very large abscess on her right rear leg, and it had been lanced and drained. For her recovery it was imperative that she orally take her antibiotics and pain medications, but Sissy had lost her appetite before treatment and had no interest in eating. We tried putting her medications in items from her usual diet, such as fish, chow, and fruits and then upgraded to peanut butter, yogurt, and ice cream, but nothing caught her interest. The way to prime a bear's appetite is through her nose, so I bought her two hot, juicy barbecued chickens from the grocery store's deli department. I was salivating just carrying them around. Their spicy, warm scent wafted into Sissy's bedroom ahead of me, and she arduously stood up and haltingly walked over to the fence to greet me—well, mostly to greet the chickens—when I got there. Success: nose and mouth running, she slowly ate one medicine-laced chicken in one sitting. Over the next two weeks, while she healed, I spent hours with her every day, keeping her company and making sure she ate her medications. She recovered well, and we formed a strong bond.

Now we were back at it. Sissy needed nursing, and I needed to figure out how to make this better for her. I crouched down and watched her. Instead of turning just her head to look at me, she stiffly turned her whole body to the right. Then she raised her left paw to her mouth and gently bit down on it, staring straight at me. As I recount in later chapters, I had observed this behavior before in other bears. I just kept watching her. She repeated the behavior several times. I believe that Sissy—like the other bears—was demonstrating that she hurt. This made perfect sense since she was recovering from several molar extractions, and the painkillers that she received in the evening were likely wearing off. The veterinarian would be coming by within the hour, so we would have to wait it out.

Maybe I could take her mind off the pain. I wondered if she had had a drink of water yet. She did have water in her automatic waterer, but she might have been too stiff to bend her head to lap water out of a dish. I got out the garden hose and adjusted it to a gentle flow of lukewarm water. Since she was locked in the room and had nowhere to go, I didn't want to force her into having to back away from the hose water if she wasn't interested in a drink, so I held the hose at my waist and let the water gently flow onto the floor near her. If she wanted to drink from it, she could just move forward and gulp water from under the stream. Instead, Sissy held her left paw under the cascade until her fur soaked up the water, and then she rubbed her face with her paw. She repeated this behavior, and I stood motionless, keeping the hose still, because it appeared that Sissy was washing.

Then, staring into my eyes, she slapped her right front leg with her left paw. It looked a little clumsy; I had no idea what she was doing, so I stood still, maintaining eye contact with her. Once again, still staring at me and without first dunking her paw in the water stream, she rubbed her front right leg with her left paw, showing me a washing motion. She completed the demonstration by again slapping her right leg. Reluctantly—in case I had misunderstood—I gently turned the hose on her right foot, which she didn't move. Again she slapped her right leg. This time I felt the message was clear—*hose the leg*. I gently hosed her right leg as she rubbed the bloody goo off with her left paw. When she was finished, she slapped her right hip with her front right paw. This time, I knew my job and gently turned the hose on her hip and rear leg.

Beginning to feel confident in my role, I got clever and slipped my thumb over the garden hose nozzle to create a fine spray, thinking that might work better for cleaning. Sissy immediately stopped washing and stared at me. Clearly I was wrong about the mist thing, so I humbly took my thumb off the nozzle; we were back to the gentle cascade, and Sissy resumed washing. I also realized my communication mistake, stopped initiating changes, and let Sissy take control.

When her right side was done, she gently slapped her fore-head with her left paw. This was a little humorous, so I smiled. I must have been too slow on the uptake, because she slapped her forehead again and expressed her mild annoyance with a pointy upper lip. Since we were communicating about hosing her head, I was again a little reluctant, so I just held the stream close to her nose. She took a step into it and let the warm water soak into her fur, envelop her head, and fall over her shoulders. And she continued to rub off the goo.

The warm water seemed to help relax her muscles, because she was now moving her head independently. Sissy tilted it up slightly and opened her mouth a crack, allowing the stream to fill her mouth with warm water. She then lowered her head and dumped out the now-pinkish water and a few red blobs of con-gealed blood. As she repeated this several times, it appeared that she was rinsing her mouth. Then Sissy turned her left side toward me, and we washed that. By this time, the veterinarian had arrived with new painkillers. Although life continued on as usual, this exchange has stayed with me; I periodically mull it over and re-enjoy the moment when I knew that Sissy and I were truly on the same page.

In any meeting between human and bear, the bear also experiences, surmises, and responds in personal ways. Bears are not in the habit of trying to please humans; they are indepen-dent and go about their business the bear way. In my opinion, they judge from their bear perspective, just as we judge from our human perspective. Can it really be any other way?

I honestly thought that Ping Pong, a very elderly, thirty-six-year-old male Asiatic black bear, had some vision left in his eyes. We knew that he had some trouble seeing but thought that he could at least see figures or shadows, since he negotiated his long-time enclosure well, albeit slowly because he was arthritic and stiff, mostly in the winter. His mate, Lailo, who was a year older than him, had some vision left. I knew this because I had begun to train her to touch her nose to my closed hand for a treat. This is the first stage of training: teaching an animal to target onto your fist or an object. From there, you can teach the animal to show you other body parts, such as paws, hips, and eyes, for veterinary purposes. I was certain that we would need the ability to check body parts, because these bears were ancient. Lailo caught on quickly and placed her nose on my fist every time to secure a treat. Ping had been watching intently— at least he was standing there intently—during my sessions with Lailo and seemed very interested.

As with Lailo, I began with Ping by gently touching my fist to his nose and then giving him a treat. To let him know at exactly what point the behavior was done accurately, I blew a small training whistle. Ping smiled his way through the first part. Now it was his turn. He had to touch his nose to my hand when I said, "Ping Pong, target." Ping waited, and I waited for him to move forward; nothing happened. I tried again: "Ping Pong, target." Nothing. Ping grew impatient, displayed a pointy upper lip, huffed, and lip-smacked a couple of times. In retrospect, I think he must have been wondering why I wasn't touching his nose and then giving him a treat. So I started over, putting my hand on his nose and then giving him a treat. He was smiling again.

About the same time that I realized that Ping was completely blind and had no idea where my fist was, he showed up for the next session with his left eye glued half shut with crusty, pudding-like gunk. A call to the veterinarian led to a quick check and a diagnosis of conjunctivitis. As he hurried out the door, the vet handed me a tiny bottle of antibiotic eye drops and told me to give these to the bear twice a day for a week. What? He had to be kidding. I looked up to ask about oral antibiotics, but the vet was gone.

At home that evening I rifled through my kitchen, looking for the perfect target. If Ping couldn't see the target, maybe he could smell it. What would soak up the smell of raw herring—Ping's favorite food—if I rubbed it on? I found it: my giant wooden spoon. The next morning, Ping and I got down to business. I said, "Ping, target" and touched his nose with the herring-smeared wooden spoon. He grabbed it and mouthed it. I grabbed it back. OK—I'd have to be quick here to get the point across. Again I said, "Ping, target," spooned his nose, and popped a grape into his mouth. Ping slowly gummed the grape—he didn't have too many teeth left—and smiled slightly, still seemingly intrigued. Again I spooned and popped. He munched and smiled. We had now laid the groundwork. Ping understood the game and held his mouth open in anticipation of the grape.

For the fourth time, I said, "Ping, target" and held the spoon a few inches away from his nose. He waited a few seconds, became impatient, huffed a bit, and then moved forward and touched the smelly spoon by himself. Instantly I erupted into an outpouring of "Good boy" compliments while cramming dozens of grapes into his mouth. He seemed a little surprised and amused as he smiled slightly between munchings. We repeated the process, and again he touched the spoon and received kudos and grapes. I held the spoon progressively farther away from his nose; he sniffed it out, touched it, and reaped his reward.

Now we were ready to deal with the initial objective, treating his infected left eye. I said, "Ping, target," held the spoon with my left hand, dropped antibiotics into his left eye with my right hand, and quick as a flash shoved grapes into his mouth, also from my right hand. It worked. Ping didn't seem concerned with the eye drops as long as there were grapes. The process wasn't elegant, and I went through about six bottles of antibiotics in one week, but it worked. Ping's eye healed. The technique was so successful that I switched Lailo over to smell targeting, too, so that I could work with them together.

I can only imagine what Ping's experience of this routine must have been like through my anthropomorphic eye. *She touches my nose with herring-scented wood, and then she gives me grapes. She stops touching my nose, and I have to find the wood myself; she gets really excited and gives me lots of grapes. I like that part; lots of grapes is good. Then we do it all again, and she drops stuff into my eye and feeds me many more grapes. Well, it's not uninteresting and there are grapes, so I guess I'll keep doing it. But where are those darn herring anyway?*

In training, it is important to keep the learning momentum going, so as treats we tend not to use food items that take a long time to chew. Grapes are perfect because they are sweet and have no refined sugars, and bears love them. I used the scent of herring on the wooden spoon because the fish smell is long lasting and pungent over a distance, and herring was Ping's favorite food.

One last note on my perspective of Ping's experience: I may well be grossly underestimating his perceptions. The scientific literature is filled with observations of animals, including bears, medicating themselves. In her book *Wild Health*, Cindy Engel reports on bears that roll in clay to treat their wounds and seek out toxic plants to annually shed their internal parasites before denning for the winter.[6] Could it be that Ping understood over time—as his eye healed—that the drops I put in made his eye feel better? Certainly the cool drops, which he presumably assumed were water, would be immediately soothing.

CHAPTER 2

THREE ROCKY
MOUNTAIN GRIZZLIES

From the Wild to Captivity

A GRIZZLY BEAR mother was escorting her cubs down a chairlift clear-cut at the Lake Louise ski area in May 1968. From below, a bird dog came charging toward them, barking. The grizzly mom tore after the dog, who ran back toward his caretaker. The bear then began running after the man instead. The man wisely kept trees between himself and the bear and escaped severe injury, sustaining one wound to his leg. After the attack, the mother bear quickly rejoined her cubs. Although later tracked and identified, the bear was allowed to go free, since the park warden felt that she had been provoked and had acted only to protect her young. A week later, she was photographed at the Lake Louise garbage dump by Stephen Herrero, a renowned bear biologist and author specializing in the causes and avoidance of bear attacks.[1] Years later, in 2005, I came across Herrero's photograph of the grizzly and the description of the attack in his book *Bear Attacks.*[2]

The grizzly bore a striking resemblance to a grizzly bear I had developed an intimate relationship with at the Calgary Zoo. Both bears had a short snout for a grizzly, gentle eyes with expressive brows, and a receding forehead. The bear I knew was aptly named Louise, since she had been brought to the zoo in September 1978 as a three-year-old rescue bear from the Chateau Lake Louise resort. Zoo staff members were told that she had grown accustomed to human food and garbage. Had she? Grizzly bears are not abundant in this area, primarily as a result of human encroachment. Because they have a low reproductive rate (less than two cubs every four and a half years),[3] they need large, undisturbed, nourishing tracts of land (about two hundred square miles for females),[4] and females do not disperse far from their natal home,[5] the female who had protected her cubs at the Lake Louise ski area was likely Louise's mother or, possibly, her grandmother. Louise may not have grown accustomed to human garbage; rather, her mother had likely shown her the best places to dine in their habitat, and this meant sometimes dining on human leftovers. Records of wild bears in the Canadian Rockies were not kept in the 1960s unless the bear had been in conflict with humans. Today, in an effort to conserve the species, most individual bears in the central Rocky Mountain ecosystem are known and are being researched.

What I found interesting about the account of the bear attack on the Lake Louise ski hill was that the grizzly bear mother had changed her course of action when she saw the human. It was the dog that had threatened her and her cubs, and the dog was clearly in retreat as she barrelled after him. The human had not charged her or her cubs, but she redirected and flew after him on sight. Did this female understand that humans are in charge of dogs and that if the human leaves, so does the dog? Or did she believe that the dog got the message and now she would give the human the same message? Perhaps she thought the dog would team up with the human to become an even greater threat, and she wanted to disperse the two. We will never know, but one thing is certain: this was a thinking bear.

I came to know Louise in 1985 and worked with her on and off for the next seventeen years. She, too, was a thinking bear. When she first arrived at the zoo, she was quarantined for thirty days to prevent the possible spread of disease to the rest of the animals. Being a young adult bear, Louise was too big for the hospital cages, so she was quarantined on exhibit. She was placed in one of the zoo's old, barred cages in what used to be called the cat-and-bear string, an area where lions, tigers, and bears were caged in a row. Each cage in the row was about one hundred square yards and had a cement floor, den, and wading pool. The fencing was made of ten-foot-tall upright iron bars, six inches apart, held together by welded horizontal bars. The top of each bar arched toward the inside of the cage to deter escape.

It didn't work. After a few days in the cage, Louise climbed up and over the top. Jim Price, an experienced large carnivore keeper, met her on the visitor path near her cage. Out of her enclosure, Louise had been confused. Where could she go? She was not on familiar terrain. Price acted quickly and called for assistance on the two-way radio while not letting Louise out of his sight. Within minutes, the veterinary crew and other staff arrived. Louise was darted unconscious and placed back into the cage.

Several weeks later, Price found Louise hanging off the inside of the fence, attempting another escape. Eventually Louise tired, loosened her grip, and slid back down the bars. Immediately after, the maintenance crew added a high-voltage hot wire to the top of the fence. That worked. Louise never escaped again.

Like the other large carnivores on the cat-and-bear string, Louise had her cage cleaned in the morning and was fed at the same time every afternoon. As in most other zoos at this time, there was not a lot of diversion in her life other than a log or two to manipulate and the wading pool. Straw bedding was generally not given to any of the animals. The high point of her day had to be the partial horse or deer carcass she was given to eat and destroy along with fruits and vegetables. But there were long hours to wait for the next feeding. So Louise, like the other large carnivores, began to pace in anticipation of cleaning in the morning and feeding in the afternoon. Eventually, the pacing bouts grew longer and extended throughout the day. Fortunately, Louise was moved to the new natural-habitat enclosure completed in July 1980.

The enclosure comprised two acres of treed land on the south slope of a hill. A stream cascaded down the crag, making one overflowing pool after another until the water congregated in a large pond at the bottom. Huge, Rocky Mountain granite boulders were embedded in the rise and dotted the underlying plain as if left by a receding glacier. The grasses grew wild except where they were disturbed by a grizzly-bear trail. The bear-holding building was on the plateau of the escarpment and was connected to the outside enclosure by a heavy-gauge mesh tunnel.

Half of the building housed two indoor bedrooms, a den, and an outdoor courtyard for the grizzly bears. The other half of the building contained an identical setup for the American black bears. Their outdoor enclosure was on the plain below the escarpment, just west of the grizzly habitat. A long wooden staircase was built into the hillside between the two enclosures for the zookeepers to use. It was hidden from view by dense brush, and it was there that I got to know Louise.

Louise was complex. She wore with grace the regal authority of an individual born to the top of her food chain. She was intelligent and in charge. Louise had an agenda and kept human and bear alike within her sphere of influence. She took responsibility for what mattered to her existence—for example, by learning the language of humans. She responded to more words, sounds, postures, and personal idiosyncrasies than any other bear I have known. She adopted the orphan cub who shared her enclosure and created and kept the balance of peace when a wild adult male grizzly joined them.

I am indebted to Louise. She taught me early in my career that a zookeeper's most important tool is relationship. Louise rewarded my attention with interaction. It was Louise who came up to the fence to greet me in the morning. It was Louise who hung around whenever zoo staff gathered to talk in her vicinity. She gave the impression of being knowledgeable. Oddly enough, it seemed that whenever the veterinary staff and I made plans in front of Louise for a procedure, Louise would change her routine and be nowhere in sight when the vet arrived the next day. I have no scientific data to back this up, but, in the interest of getting the job done, I did stop making plans in front of her.

Clearly, Louise was cueing on something.

Louise lived with a young female grizzly bear named Khutzeymateen, after the Khutzeymateen Valley in the northern

British Columbia rain forest wilderness. At Khutzy's birth in 1990 at the Calgary Zoo, the protection of the valley and the grizzlies in it was a hotly contested issue in the province, in the country, and around the world. Khutzy's caregiver, Bob Klassen, a long-time carnivore keeper, named her in honor of the struggle. In 1994 the Khutzeymateen Grizzly Bear Sanctuary was established and officially opened by His Royal Highness Prince Philip, Duke of Edinburgh.

Khutzy's existence was an accident. It was not the Calgary Zoo's intent to breed grizzly bears. Because of the zoo's proximity to the Rocky Mountains, its mandate has always been to rescue grizzlies that come into conflict with humans. Both of Khutzy's parents were barren-ground grizzly bears rescued by the Canadian Wildlife Service from the Canadian Northwest Territories. Barren-ground grizzlies are Arctic-dwelling brown bears that are usually smaller, but no less tough, than Rocky Mountain grizzlies. The weight for females in spring, which is their leanest time of year, can be as little as 250 pounds and for males can be as low as 300 pounds.[6] In comparison, weights for Rocky Mountain grizzlies in the Banff and Lake Louise area range from 330 to 440 pounds for females and 550 to 880 pounds for males.[7]

Khutzy's mother, Florence, was twenty-six years old when she bred with a male named Curly (after the tufts of blond fur curling around his ears). Because of Florence's advanced age, she was thought to be past her reproductive years and was not given birth control, as most animals in a mixed group were.

In the fall of 1989, Florence meticulously gathered up grasses, leaves, twigs, and branches from the enclosure and made herself a nest in the earthen den on the hillside. She and other grizzlies had excavated the den over the years, but that year, Florence took ownership of it. On March 21, 1990, Klassen heard a cub crying in the den. A few weeks later, Khutzy, a tiny caramel-colored fluffball, made her public debut, with her proud mother holding her head high in the enclosure.

As Klassen and the relief keeper soon found out, the five-pound cub was small enough to get through the three-by-six-inch mesh and cause a huge ruckus. She could get out but was not yet wise enough to get back in, causing her frantic mother to run up and down the fence line huffing and woofing, pawing through the fence to get to her cub. As a short-term solution the zookeeper would scoop up the little cub, sometimes having to rip through the dense brush to get to her, and push her back through the mesh. It wasn't difficult to find Khutzy, even if she got out overnight. Florence never took her eyes off the baby. A second, finer-gauge mesh was tied onto the first to cub-proof the fence and alleviate everyone's trauma.

Florence, an old bear, was inclined to be a doting, protective, and indulgent mother. It wasn't until early summer that Louise was allowed to join the mother and cub. Louise was curious but kept a respectful distance from the cub, a behavior reinforced by Florence's huffy warnings. For the next five years, the three lived together. Khutzy was the apple of her mother's eye and the focal point of attention of her aunt Louise and adoring zookeepers. Over time, Florence began to show the signs of an aging bear. She moved her hind quarters slowly and stiffly and with care, as if in arthritic pain, often backing up the steep hill, probably to take the pressure off of her sore rear joints and muscles. On September 15, 1995, life changed inalterably for Khutzy when Florence died.

Khutzy was five years old. If Florence had raised Khutzy in the wild, Khutzy would have been expelled from her mother's company at the age of two or three, depending on how much food was available or if a male suitor was otherwise occupying her mother's attention. This is an extremely stressful and dangerous time for young adults in the wild, since they then have to fend for themselves. If they hadn't paid attention during their mother's instruction, they would pay for it then. Often, cubs stay with their siblings or form protective groups with other young adults.[8] In the captive environment, it is not unusual for a young adult to not fully mature in attitude while living with her parent beyond the normal period of dispersion. There had been no life-threatening challenges in Khutzy's life to teach her how to survive in crisis and fend for herself.

At Florence's death, Louise adopted Khutzeymateen. Louise behaved like Florence, allowing Khutzy to eat the better foods, which Khutzy sometimes took right out of Louise's mouth. Louise would huff to Khutzy to come out of stormy weather and to move away from loud, sputtering snow blowers or any other perceived threats. Khutzy continued in the cub role, bounding carefree around the enclosure, looking to Louise for direction.

The death of Florence could have been traumatic enough to catapult the immature Khutzy into serious adulthood. But instead, Louise stepped in, responded to the cublike behavior, and took over. Acting as Khutzy's mother offered Louise an opportunity to control this otherwise adult bear and to be at the top of the hierarchy. But this mother-and-daughter arrangement also offered mental stimulation. Louise had a purpose and something significant to occupy her time with in her relatively unchanging environment. Khutzy allowed this behavior, likely because it was a quick and easy solution to the crisis of losing her mother. It was what Khutzy knew. Losing Florence brought instability and challenge to her world. Khutzy would have had to stand up to another female bear, something that she had never done before and likely did not have the skill to do. Louise's maternal behavior acted as an offered olive branch and brought stability once again to Khutzy's world.

Louise appeared content in her role. She beamed the broad smile of a proud parent, staying close by as she watched me give Khutzy treats and attention through the fence. It was in my interest to work with Louise and Khutzy as mother and daughter.

It was management practice to lock all dangerous animals in their buildings overnight as a precautionary measure against intoxicated or misguided human trespassers who had plans to jump in with them. From a human safety perspective the practice made sense, but it did not serve the animals well. It meant that the bears only had access to the large enclosure for eight to sixteen hours, depending on when the zoo closed for the day. I didn't like the practice much, and neither did Khutzy.

Louise understood the routine and usually came in, unless it was an exceptionally beautiful, sunny day with warm winds blowing scents of information through the enclosure fence. I bribed her by offering dinner, enriching treats, and fresh bedding material in the building. Khutzy, the overgrown cub, didn't care; she wanted to run free in the large enclosure, where, as she demonstrated, she preferred to play in the pools, roll in the dirt, and climb logs. I could call her name until I had the attention of every creature in the zoo except for Khutzy. I tried many tactics, showing her treats to be had if she came in or pretending to play catch-me, catch-me, all the while working the game up the hill, over to and through the tunnel, only to have Khutzy shoot back out like a cartoon cannonball when I tried to close the gate.

One late afternoon I couldn't find Khutzy anywhere in the enclosure. Losing the whereabouts of a large carnivore tends to make a zookeeper a little nervous. "Where's Khutzy?" I was frustrated, and I was being facetious when I asked Louise as she walked past me in the tunnel. I wasn't expecting a response. To my great surprise, Louise stopped, turned around, and stared down the hill at a large rock. Instinctively my eyes followed her nose, pointing out her line of sight, and there was Khutzy lying behind a large boulder—wide awake—hiding.

How had Louise understood my question? Louise knew that the human sound *Khutzy* indicated Khutzy the bear, much as two pet dogs in one household know each other's names. I can only guess that the intonation of my voice, the frustration exhibited in my body language, and the time of day expressed my need to find the little rogue bear. I praised Louise by telling her "Good girl!" and hiked back down the hill, as close to the boulder as I could get from the opposite side of the fence. I flushed out Khutzy by calling her name and staring at her, registering my complaint. Khutzy stood up from behind the rock, hung her head, and flattened her ears against her back in annoyance. Refusing to make eye contact with me, she sauntered up the hill and into the tunnel as I closed the gate behind her.

In the days that followed, Khutzy repeatedly attempted to hide, and each time Louise would point her out at my request. Exposed, Khutzy would grudgingly come in, head hanging, ears lying flat, refusing to make eye contact with either Louise or me. Khutzy must have given this disagreeable routine some thought, because one afternoon she stopped coming in after I flushed her out of hiding. She had finally understood that I couldn't make her do anything she didn't want to. I was frustrated and jokingly said to Louise, "Go get Khutzy," as I looked in Khutzy's direction. Again, I wasn't expecting a response, and again, I was surprised. Louise looked at me, exhaled heavily like a weary human, and trudged back down the hill. She flushed Khutzy out from behind a bush and herded her up the hill, nipping at her heels all the way into the tunnel. I praised Khutzy for coming in—as if she'd had a choice. She ignored me and kept walking, head hanging, ears flat, no eye contact. Louise followed and stopped when she got to me. Astounded by what had just happened, I thanked her profusely and gave her lots of praise. Louise smiled and moved on.

After that day I asked Louise to get Khutzy whenever she wouldn't come in on her own. Louise would look in Khutzy's direction, exhale a heavy sigh, and then herd the cub up the hill. I wondered about that sigh. It never felt as though Louise was frustrated by my request; rather, she seemed annoyed with Khutzy.

Why did Louise help me? She would certainly receive her food and rewards for coming in regardless of Khutzy's whereabouts. You cannot make one animal responsible for the actions of another. If Khutzy stayed out for the night, I would leave the gate open between the two bears so that Louise would remain within reach of Khutzy. Louise may have had a sense of orderliness, a sort of *we always do it this way* reasoning, but, in my experience, that attitude is unusual in bears, who are generally responsive to what is happening immediately around them. I came to understand Louise's assistance as an act of benevolence.

Louise and I became friends. I treated Khutzy as her cub and Louise as the bear in charge. She always had a personal agenda, which she would repeatedly attempt to communicate to me. If I missed the point du jour, she would let me know, often by pooping in her automatic water dish, leaving a disgusting soupy mess. This proved to be an effective mode of communication, since I would invariably turn my attention to her behavior for clarification on the issue.

Bears have rudimentary verbal language. A specific sound can signify a number of messages. The verbal message is further honed and supported by accompanying body language. For instance, a short, soft huff can mean *I'm over here*. If this is expressed by a bear lying behind a rock, head up, looking straight at you, it can mean *I'm over here; what do you want?* If the huff is accompanied by a pointy upper lip, the meaning could be *I'm over here, and I'm annoyed*. But, if the *I'm over here* huff is expressed by a bear lying behind a rock, keeping her head low, body scrunched together, smiling broadly while sneaking peeks at another bear, it could mean *I'm over here, and I'm hiding but not from you; I'm having fun*. Like humans, bears communicate mostly through body language and inference.

A bear will get another animal's attention using verbal language but express meaning by demonstration. When I gave treats to Louise and Khutzy at the fence, Louise would allow Khutzy to have treats first. When she wanted one, she would pick up her front paw, move it toward me, and put it down again several times, effectively patting the ground, meaning *I want it here, now*. If I missed her paw action, she would express a soft huff to get my attention and pat the ground again. Humans, bears, and other mammals often share the same body language. If a human wants his dog to come up and sit next to him on the couch, he gets the dog's attention verbally—"Fido!"—then pats the area next to him on the couch, meaning, *Come and sit here, Fido.*

At times, I felt Louise overestimated my knowledge or sphere of influence. On several occasions a bright sunny morning would turn to rain in the time it took me to clean the large enclosure and put down enriching activities like puzzle feeders. Louise was unaware of the change in weather, since she had been temporarily locked in the building. When I opened the gate and unveiled the change in weather, her hanging head, pointy upper lip, and sideways glance gave me the impression that the rain was, well, my fault.

Louise allowed me to train Khutzy without interfering. In order for me to work safely with the bears at the fence, it was essential that each bear learn not to put her paws through the mesh. It took three lessons for Khutzy to learn the no paws rule. I would reward her with food treats for sitting with both front paws on the ground. If she put her paw through the mesh to help herself to treats or to touch me, I would say, "Khutzy, no paws" and withdraw my attention. I would praise her for pulling back her paws. The first time I did this, Khutzy thought my response was incidental. The second time it happened, she saw that there was a pattern. The third time, she tested the theory— could I really mean for her not to stick her paws through the mesh? Yes, I meant it. Once she understood the concept, she would periodically test my resolve.

My role with Khutzy was most often that of maid service and chairman of the entertainment committee. I and the animal care volunteers that worked with me spent a lot of time playing with her. She loved to run up and down along the fence in hot pursuit of a human. And she loved to play tug-o'-war. Bears who are given enriching things to do every day generally do not eat nonfood items like cardboard, paper, plastic containers, or leather. They don't need to experience the daylights out of any one item to stimulate their brain. So I would play tug-o'-war with Khutzy using one of my leather gloves, knowing that I would inevitably lose the glove to her.

On one particularly cold day, I stuck an empty glove-finger through the mesh, fishing for a tug-o'-war partner. Khutzy took the bait immediately, and we struggled back and forth. Khutzy was never in the mood to let me win—she loved to win—so she pulled hard, and I had to juggle my body weight to avoid being slammed into the bars. Since it was at least minus thirteen degrees Farenheit that afternoon, I had my jacket sleeve down over my bare right hand, which was holding the glove. My left hand was gloved, in a pocket, and out of sight. In less than two minutes, I had no strength left to hang onto the glove and let go, causing Khutzy to lose her balance and step backward. In the second that it took for her to renegotiate her balance, I had slipped my bare hand into a pocket to keep it warm. Unaware, Khutzy beamed and began her bouncing *I won and you lost* dance, swinging the glove around in her mouth. Suddenly she froze on the spot. All of the joy washed from her face as she starred at my right arm. My hand wasn't visible. Instinctively, I pulled my hand out of the pocket and showed it to her, front and back. Seeing it firmly affixed to my forearm, she resumed her shameless victory boogie.

Khutzy was afraid that she had torn my hand off along with the glove, or so I thought, but I wanted to test my understanding. Before I shared my opinion, I asked Matt Wort and Sue

Vestre, the two animal care volunteers who were with me, what they thought had just happened. Both had immediately felt the same thing, that Khutzy was afraid that she had hurt me and that when she saw my hand she was relieved. I was overwhelmed and felt truly honored that this little bear seemed to care whether my hand was still on my arm. That feeling was mixed with a more professional recognition that thankfully Khutzy was beginning to care about things other than herself. She was slowly maturing, despite the odds.

In August 1996, Khutzy's life was again unalterably changed. This time neither Louise nor the zookeepers would come to Khutzy's rescue, and nothing would ever be the same. A huge, wild male grizzly bear was about to force her to mature in a hurry.

A TINY, ONE-POUND male bear cub was born in the eastern slopes of the Canadian Rocky Mountains in the winter of 1990. His second year with his mother was a tough one, since the wild berry crop had failed. As a young adult of three years, he had left his mother and established a home range in the Bow Valley region of the mountains spanning part of Alberta and British Columbia. If his behavior had not had such dire consequences to his life, his wild exploits would sound like the modern-day adventures of Yogi Bear without Boo Boo. This male caused a commotion wherever he went. He was often the focal point of bear jams in the park when visitors parked their cars and got out to photograph him as he grazed peaceably by the side of the road, ignoring up to twenty people at a time. Although he was extremely tolerant, occasionally he felt the need to bluff-charge an admirer who came too close. In 1993, he raided an illegal campground near Castle Junction and ate the campers' food. He was caught and collared. From then on he became known to the park staff as Bear 16—his tag number.

Bear 16 was spotted at the side of the railway tracks feeding off grain spills from Canadian Pacific Railway cars that were being transported from Saskatchewan west through the Rockies to the British Columbia coast. On one occasion he was entertaining a crowd by playing with a dog toy near Castle Junction. Park wardens targeted him with negative reinforcement, using rubber bullets and bear bangers (noise makers used to scare off bears). But Bear 16 was undaunted, and the older he got, the bolder he got.

In 1996, he wandered into the towns of Field and Lake Louise in broad daylight. He stuck his nose through the open door of Laggan's Mountain Bakery and Deli at Samson Mall in Lake Louise. He bluff-charged two vehicles parked at the side of the road and two people fishing at Wapta Lake. When a grizzly stepped on a tent and accidentally on the camper in the tent, Bear 16 was also considered the likely suspect. This proved to be his last hurrah. Park wardens got tough, and he was relocated to the remote end of his home range. It had already been decided that if he came back, he would have to be either completely removed from the ecosystem or shot. Remarkably, Bear 16 hiked through three mountain passes in deep snow and returned to the Bow Valley in just four days.

Reluctant to shoot such a determined, extraordinary bear, park wardens made a phone call to the Calgary Zoo, and Bear 16 got a new home. True to his legacy, this move, too, was not without controversy. To live at the zoo with Louise and Khutzy, Bear 16 would have to be vasectomized. This decision caused a stirring of public emotion, since his genetic contribution to the wild population would be lost forever. It was a sobering moment, but the procedure was necessary since the Calgary Zoo acted to house rescue bears, not to breed them.

After thirty days in the hospital quarantine facility, Bear 16 was sedated and moved in a cargo net in the hospital van, accompanied by several veterinary staff and an entourage of zookeepers to help carry his limp, eight-hundred-pound body from the vehicle into the bear building. He was put on the cement floor in the bedroom that was adjacent to the outside enclosure via the mesh tunnel. The room was like a cage, with three cinderblock walls and a barred front. The ceiling was protected with heavy-gauge mesh to keep the bears from breaking the skylight and crawling out.

I was working with an inexperienced zookeeper and, as is customary for recovering animals, we kept vigil over Bear 16 until he woke up. A few hours after his arrival, he was acutely aware of his surroundings. I had locked Louise and Khutzy into the large enclosure, away from Bear 16, but they could smell him and they weren't happy. Mother and daughter stood at utmost attention, motionless, side by side like a wall of bristled fur, ears lying back on their heads, eyes and snout focused on the bedroom door.

Although Bear 16 could not see Louise and Khutzy, he could smell them. He knew he was on another bear's turf. The fact that they were female was of no comfort in these close quarters. He was huge and filled the tiny bedroom with his girth. He wanted out! He bounced from corner to corner of the room with his front paws, off the metal bars, testing them to see if he could escape. It would be better for Bear 16 to see the bears outside than to guess at who they were and how many there were. I opened the gate. Bear 16 stared directly at Louise and Khutzy across the way. They looked tough and seriously unamused. This was their territory. Bear 16 was the interloper, and he knew it. Bear 16 was standing in the doorway, the front half of his body outside and the rear half inside. The front half looked tough, fur bristled, standing its ground. The rear half, which faced me, was shaking, urinating, and defecating diarrhea all over himself, the floor, and the walls. The air reeked of excrement and bear sweat.

Bear 16 made a decision. He was outta there! He backed into the bedroom and rammed the bars where I was standing. They held. He looked wildly around, then looked up and saw the skylight covered with mesh. Next came one of those moments, when time slows down, that a zookeeper never forgets. Bear 16 stood up on his hind legs, grabbed onto the ceiling mesh with his front paws, hoisted himself up—all eight hundred pounds of him—and hung off the ceiling mesh on all fours. The mesh began to buckle under. I caught a glimpse of the new zookeeper, whose face was the color of wallpaper paste. I sent her outside until I could get the bear off the ceiling. I opened the gates to the courtyard and the second bedroom. He dropped off the ceiling and shot out the side door on a kamikaze run. He did not understand that the girls were locked away from him.

I called the animal hospital. Having no real time for details, I quickly described the behavior and asked for some calming medication so that Bear 16 could be more safely acclimated to the new surroundings. The veterinary technician wanted to know what I was doing to that bear, since he had been fine in hospital quarantine. Good point, but they had not been in the unenviable position of having to coax a wild male bear into the living quarters of other adult bears. We got our drugs, but the worst was over, and I chose not to use them. Bear 16 had come to the conclusion that Louise and Khutzy were not able to get at him, and so he began a meticulous inspection of the building and the courtyard for weaknesses.

That night I wondered how this would ever work. Tomorrow began a daunting task. I had to convince a wild male bear that he was to share this relatively small enclosure with two other adult bears. This request obviously flew in the face of Bear 16's wild experience, which told him to move away from the angry mother with the equally angry adult cub. What I understood clearly was that I had no way of communicating with him; he was a wild bear that had had only a brief introduction to captive culture at the animal hospital. Even simple acts such as my opening and closing gates startled him to the point that he would punch the gate in anger.

We needed to start at the beginning. I had to be able to get his attention in a relatively consistent manner so that he and I could develop a relationship. We would take one step at a time. Tomorrow's lesson would be name recognition. George Halmazna, an animal care foreman, renamed Bear 16 Skoki after the expansive and remarkable Skoki Valley in the bear's old home range.

In the morning, both Skoki and I were tired. Judging by the mess of food, feces, and bedding on the floor, Skoki had been restless and had been trying to leave overnight. I moved slowly in his presence and spoke softly and soothingly, I hoped. Teaching Skoki his name involved treats. Whenever he responded to the sound Skoki, even if just his ears moved in my direction, I would toss him a treat. When you are teaching a bear a critical concept, it is imperative that your reward be worth the effort of learning.

Now was no time to be health conscious or cheap. On my way to work, I bought several bags of hyperpuffed marshmallows, which are regarded as a prize by captive bears since they are so sweet and full of calories. Skoki took the first marshmallow in his mouth, tested it, and spit it out. This wild bear did not seem to have a sweet tooth, or he didn't recognize marshmallows as a food. I resorted to meat treats such as chunks of horsemeat and herring, foods that Louise and Khutzy generally considered same old, same old. This worked for Skoki. The objective of the treat was to reward him for a concept understood or a behavior done when it occurred. If he were given chunks of meat every time he responded, the eating process would impede the learning process. I experimented and found that Skoki loved grapes. Then the learning began in earnest.

Whenever Skoki was in the courtyard watching the girls, I would go to the large enclosure fence and call Louise and Khutzy's names. Then I would reward them for coming up and for not showing signs of aggression toward Skoki. It was difficult to catch them in the act of being peaceable, as Khutzy bit the bars, bared her teeth, clawed in the dirt, and slammed the fence, while Louise, grievously concerned about her cub's welfare, spit huffing threats, gnashed her teeth, and hurled stares at Skoki. The girls looked every bit like the killers that I knew they would be if challenged. Their focus and behaviors changed slightly when I brought out a bag of marshmallows—I knew they would be more effective than grapes, which they received all the time. Louise and Khutzy could not believe their good treat fortune.

These training sessions served two purposes. One, Skoki would learn that each bear responded to a certain sound—her name—and would get food for it. Two, if I continued to bribe

the girls with marshmallows, they would learn to behave better around Skoki and perhaps even forgive me for bringing this
nasty male into their lives. By watching my interaction with
the girls, Skoki learned to come when I called his name.

After Skoki spent a few days getting to know the building
and courtyard, it was time to introduce him to the large enclosure. This was prime real estate, and the girls were not going to
like being relegated to the building and courtyard just to
accommodate Skoki's education. It was crucial that Skoki
become familiar with the entire facility before any introductions could be considered. Such knowledge would even out the
playing field, would lower Skoki's stress level and assist him in
making graceful exits if need be during the introductions.
Louise was no shrinking violet; she was one tough, smart
mama bear who needed to stay in charge above all else to protect her adopted cub. And we couldn't allow this massive male
to run the show, because he was too big and could easily kill
one or both of the girls.

Fortunately it was August, the extreme tail end of breeding
season. At the height of breeding season, there is too much
energy and hormone-charged anxiety to accomplish a smooth
introduction. At the end of the season, bears are still in the meet-
and-greet mode but are better able to maintain a mellow attitude
toward the opposite sex.

Much to their annoyance, I shifted Louise and Khutzy to the
building and courtyard and gave Skoki access to the large enclosure. He did not waste any time. He ran into the enclosure over
to the upper falls and leapt into the pool. He lay there on his
back for the rest of the day, like a couch potato in a Barkalounger,
with his legs in the air. I assumed that he was exploring the

enclosure at night, because every morning I found him in the pool, and he stayed there all day.

I lost temporary control over him. As expected, Skoki would no longer come when I called. His new environment was better than grapes. He was enjoying what must have seemed like a reprieve from the very restricted world he had found himself in. So I stopped trying. I decided to sit by the fence and keep him company.

CHAPTER 3

SEX AND THE SINGLE GRIZZLY

Skoki Moves In

As THE DAYS passed, Louise and Khutzy became even less fond of this giant male bear who had exiled them from the pools, stream, trees, and grassy hillside in the outside enclosure. Louise spent much of her time standing motionless at the closed tunnel gate, waiting to catch a glimpse of Skoki's activities. It was difficult for her to spot him, because she could not see beyond the precipice of the hill's summit. Periodically, she would leave the tunnel gate to peer through the courtyard fence, hanging her head and huffing and jaw snapping at no one that I could see. Khutzy spent some of her time standing right behind Louise in the tunnel also watching for Skoki and annoying Louise. The two would then exchange huffing and guttural vocals, wrinkle their snouts, and display their teeth to each other. Nobody was happy except Skoki.

I had to regain some control over Skoki's movement so I that could alternate access to the enclosure between him and the girls. If the current situation went on for much longer, the animosity between the girls and Skoki might be hard to overcome when they were eventually introduced. To make myself accessible to Skoki, I sat for hours by the fence of the large enclosure, near the pool that he lounged in. If he wanted to visit with me, he could—and he did. After five days, he came over, sniffed around the ground, and glanced at me quickly from the corner of his eye while he was "busy" sniffing small sticks and raking other minuscule things on the ground.

Skoki was huge. At well over eight hundred pounds, he was twice Khutzy's size and an additional one-third the size of Louise. Looking into his face, I didn't know this bear, and part of me was scared. I logically understood that there was a fence between us and that he could not hurt me, but he was huge, well armed, and unknown. Even experienced zookeepers feel this awe, respect, and self-consciousness. You feel smaller somehow, vulnerable in the face of an unknown, or sometimes known, large carnivore. It's a humbling, primal feeling that makes cell phones, water bottles, jogging suits, high-speed Internet, and all other necessities of modern existence utterly irrelevant. You'd have to be dead to your own instincts to not feel it. Skoki and I had to develop a relationship in order for this arrangement to work out for Skoki and the girls.

As I sat there watching, Skoki sorted bits of natural junk on the ground while he watched me. I'd throw to him grapes, apples, herring, or whatever I had to bribe my way into his confidence again. Looking at me, he would slowly, gracefully pick up the item with his lips, then inhale, crush, and swallow it. On several occasions he quietly, softly worked his way over to the fence, slammed it full force with his paw right near my head, and watched me jump as bits of nature flew from his paws and rained down over me. Sometimes he was smiling; sometimes he wasn't. I only jumped the first time and learned to anticipate his sudden displays of aggression. Then he resorted to bluff charges. He'd quietly move away from the fence, seeming to mind his own business, then turn instantly and charge like a stampeding buffalo—huffing and leading with his forehead—stopping abruptly only yards from the fence, plowing soil, and kicking up dirt. He was never smiling when he was in a full-blown bluff charge. He could have been telling me to leave him alone, but his charges were not persistent. He could have been showing me his frustration at being in this situation, enclosed in an environment that was clearly occupied by two other grizzly bears—a point that was well taken. He could have been testing my mettle.

I could have removed myself from the situation, as animal-training procedures often dictate in the face of aggressive behavior. This action shows the animal that aggressive behavior is not tolerated, since the treats leave along with the person. But I wasn't training him in procedures. We were communicating, building a relationship. Bears communicate in large part by demonstration. If I had left every time he demonstrated meaning through aggression, the conversation would have been only half stated. I wanted Skoki to think that I was worth befriending like any other bear, that I wouldn't leave halfway through a conversation. Within a couple of days, his bluff charges grew less intense and less well defined. If he found himself at a distance from me, he might turn and run or speed-walk toward me, then stop abruptly to eat treats or feign interest in the ground and smile, glancing my way. The worst seemed to be over. After those two days of aggressive interaction, he never bluff-charged or slammed the fence at my head again.

Skoki now came up to the fence and allowed me to hand-feed him. When the treats were gone, he would remain sitting or lying next to me. I began to call him from the top of the hill to come into the building, and he would. I let him come and go a few times, and then I closed the gate behind him. He seemed to take this in stride, showing more interest in the straw and foods I had laid out for him in the building.

Much to Louise and Khutzy's relief, they could now go out into the enclosure. It had been almost ten days since they had last been there. They had serious work to do, as they meticulously sniffed the ground, sticks, and rocks, rolled over logs, and raked soil and grass, collecting information at every location where Skoki had spent time.

It was getting to be late August, the absolute tail end of grizzly bear breeding season. Unless you want to breed bears, which we did not, it is best to introduce bears to each other during the very end of their normal breeding season, while they are still in the meet-and-greet mode. Introducing bears that simply have to live together during the height of breeding season can cause a needlessly intense, hormonal fervor of aggressive behavior.

Skoki was coming when I called him and shifting when I needed him to. Louise and Khutzy were getting used to sharing spaces with Skoki. They were no longer spending hours at the fence waiting for him to pass by so that they could bluff-charge, huff, or make faces at him. They were going about their daily routine of eating, building their nests, sorting through enrichment objects, and napping. It was time to put them all together.

Grizzly bears are independent individuals. There is very little that is retiring or withdrawn in the personality of a mentally and physically healthy grizzly bear. Females and males alike are entirely self-sufficient, resourceful, and opportunistic. They have only two motivators: food and reproduction, in that order. Bears care about food all of the time and about reproduction some of time. If you want to be successful at introducing grizzly bears to each other, you have to address these two motivators and how they relate to each particular animal at the time of introduction.

Louise cared about food for herself and for Khutzy. Khutzy cared about food for herself. Her imperious status was reinforced by Louise, who, in the maternal role, allowed Khutzy to have treats from keepers first while Louise sat and watched, usually with a broad smile under her nose.

Skoki cared about food for himself—enough food. He was a big animal, with an immediate need to get bigger, as fall was around the corner. Like other grizzlies, he was busy ingesting as many calories as possible to put on the extra fat he would need to get him through not only the winter's denning period but also the early spring, when there still wasn't much food available.

Before we could put the bears into the same enclosure, we had to convince them that there would be enough food for all of their fall-induced appetites. So we greatly increased their diets. We measured omnivore chow by the garbage-can full and gave them boxes of apples, carrots, and kale. They got whole melons and berries—whatever we had, including potatoes, peanuts, and raisins. We went along the Bow River and cut fresh willow and cottonwood branches for them. From the commissary we ordered buckets of herring, mackerel, occasionally salmon, whole chickens and rabbits, horsemeat, and bones to chew on.

These foods were generously scattered on the ground and put into puzzle feeders, hidden in straw piles, under logs, and in paper bags and boxes three to four times a day. In addition to the usual fall increase in foods, we increased their diet enormously one week before the introductions. We wanted to make the point that this increase in food was not fleeting but was a serious, permanent change. Adult bears can tolerate each other better when there is no food shortage. Grizzly bears will gobble up juicy, egg-rich fish within plain sight of each other at salmon spawning grounds in British Columbia, respecting each other's personal space—a sort of portable mini-territory. When Louise, Khutzy, and Skoki were put together, I hoped the females would understand that there was no need to drive off the new bear to secure food resources.

Louise was the obvious first choice to meet Skoki. She was an experienced female who had lived and bred with males before. Introducing Skoki to Khutzy first wouldn't be fair to Khutzy, since she had zero skills in meeting anyone new, never mind a male twice her size.

Introducing grizzly bears to each other is a serious event in a zoo, especially introducing a wild bear to a long-time captive bear. That day we had plenty of staff on hand, holding primed fire hoses and carbon dioxide canisters to break up a fight. Foremen and keepers had observed and discussed the behavior of Louise and Skoki toward each other across the fence. The two had become quite cordial, even peaceable. If they had continued to show aggression, we would not have introduced them.

On the morning of Louise's introduction to Skoki, they were both fed as much food as they wanted. The golden rule of bear introductions is to never, ever introduce one hungry bear to another hungry bear and expect it to go well. We also enriched the large enclosure with lots of scattered foods. Bears need items to pretend to investigate while they consider their options in the face of a minor threat. It's a great way to appear unconcerned until you develop a plan of action—a sort of displacement behavior. People do it too. Why do we avert our eyes and check our watches or cell phones when we discover that we are being looked at by another human in a crowd? It gives us that moment we need to decide what to do with the other person's attention.

I gave Louise access to the large enclosure first and kept Khutzy in the building. This was a diversion from the normal morning routine, and the girls immediately knew something was up. Louise got busy checking and testing the foods in the enclosure. I then gave Skoki access to the tunnel. He had watched from the courtyard as I let Louise in, so he knew she was out there. Skoki sat next to me in the tunnel by the gate. Up until now, I had kept the bears separated from each other. I can only imagine that Skoki had been counting on my good sense to do that again today. I gave Louise the heads-up that I was opening the gate and I looked at Skoki, who was sitting staring at the gate; he seemed to have some level of understanding of what might happen next.

It was time; I opened the gate. Louise had come up the hill. With the gate wide open and Louise staring directly at him— for a split second—Skoki turned his head and looked directly into my eyes. He was dark, serious, and concerned. I had proven not to be trustworthy. I felt accused. Then he thundered forward into the enclosure, facing off with Louise. With deafening growls, snapping, jaws, and flying spit, their fur standing on end, they began dancing around each other like prize fighters on four legs, then two, paws punching air. But they made no contact. They separated, paced in their own corners, burning up adrenaline. Again Louise lunged forward, spit running in rivers from her open mouth through massive teeth, backing up Skoki. Skoki mirrored her stance. But there was no contact.

This is what I was counting on. Grizzly bears will argue, sometimes extensively, so that the entire mountainside can hear them, but they prefer not to make contact unless they absolutely have to. They are well-armed, powerful animals who can't afford to physically fight with other grizzlies, because they can do each other serious harm.

Throughout the next few days, Louise and Skoki had a few argumentative skirmishes, which decreased in length and intensity. I had given Khutzy access to the courtyard from the building during the introduction. Although she was hopping around at the fence, fur on end, growling and huffing at the sight of Louise and Skoki negotiating, it was vital that she watch and learn from them. Soon it would be her turn.

Skoki was subtle as he changed his tactics with Louise. He began to follow her around wherever she went. Although it was late in the season, Skoki was courting Louise, and she knew it. She would huff, snap her jaws, and move a few steps toward Skoki, and he would back up—slightly. Her aggressive responses were brief, although they could be huffy and occasionally work into fuller-blown arguments. But Skoki patiently persisted. Louise showed periodic interest in Khutzy's whereabouts but generally ignored her calls for attention from the courtyard.

A week later, we introduced Khutzy into the mix, hoping that Skoki was so intent on pursuing his tryst with Louise that he and Louise would pretty much ignore Khutzy after their initial, inevitable deliberations. On the morning of Khutzy's introduction, all the bears ate a huge breakfast of omnivore chow, fruit, and fish. We gave Louise and Skoki access to the large enclosure. While they busied themselves with food and each other, I moved Khutzy into the tunnel. This is what she had been waiting for. I gave Louise and Skoki the heads-up that I was opening the gate. Khutzy knew what that meant. When I opened the gate, Khutzy torpedoed out of the tunnel, passed Louise, who was coming up the hill to greet her, and aimed directly for Skoki. Unlike what Louise had done with Skoki, Khutzy made a direct hit, head on, and a fight ensued. It was clear that Khutzy had not used her week wisely. There was no skill or finesse here—she was making it up as she went along.

Skoki backed up continuously, trying to shake off this small, obnoxious bear. He checked behind himself periodically, presumably making sure he wasn't being cornered. He could have killed Khutzy but clearly chose not to. He seemed confused by her behavior and constantly tried to sidestep her. Louise defended her precious, overgrown cub by flanking Skoki, drowning him in noisy guttural protests, and snapping her jaws. Skoki retreated, with Khutzy in pursuit. Khutzy noticed that Louise was not following to back her up, so when Skoki turned again to face Khutzy, Khutzy retreated to sit in the pond.

Wildlife biologists have observed males courting females with cubs. Generally, two-year-old cubs hide in the brush, periodically making themselves known by approaching their mother, only to run off at the slightest provocation.[1] The female ignores them, and eventually they disappear. Adult bears also seem to move off the breeding grounds of an engaged pair.[2]

So where did Khutzy's behavior fit into Skoki's understanding? Khutzy's perennially immature cublike behavior—supersized now that she was an adult—might seem, at the very least, a little unusual to Skoki's experience with wild bears. Skoki focused on breeding with Louise. The couple continued with their ritual; he followed her, and she objected less and less as time passed. Eventually, Skoki and Louise began sleeping in the near vicinity of each other and eating together.

Khutzy would flit around the couple, desperately trying to get their attention. She'd swing her head back and forth a few times (an invitation to play), playfully bite Louise on the heel of her foot when she was resting with Skoki, run around them in quick semicircles in exaggerated bouncy motions, and take toys, logs, or rocks to Louise. When these antics failed to get attention, she'd pick a fight with Skoki by side-checking him or coming too close to food he was showing interest in. Once, she just walked right over him as if he weren't lying there on the ground. In these little skirmishes, Skoki usually retreated by backing off or moving away.

Clearly, Khutzy had mistaken kindness for weakness. One day Skoki was making his way down the hill by climbing over the boulders. Khutzy charged up the hill, bouncing off rocks as she accelerated, and met Skoki head-on. Standing motionless, Skoki stared down at this small, in-his-face, jaw-snapping, drooling bear. He must have had enough. With lightning speed, he cuffed Khutzy with his right paw, hooked her under her chin, and flipped her backwards down the hill. She rolled like a ball, bouncing off rocks until she hit bottom. That had to hurt, even if you were insulated with fat. Hanging her head, Khutzy got up slowly, did not look back up the hill, and haltingly walked over to the pond and got into it. She sat there with her back to Skoki, submerged up to her head, for the rest of the day.

I thought this incident would be one of Khutzy's great life lessons and that she would not bother Skoki anymore. Not so!

It was late in the afternoon. I had come back to check on the grizzlies before I went home. As had become her new habit, Khutzy came up to the fence to commiserate with me. She would sit on her haunches, slump her shoulders, hang her head, and sadly, slowly, take well-loved treats from my hand between her lips and somberly chew on them. Life pretty much sucked. Louise and Skoki were busy with each other, and no one paid any attention to Khutzy. She seemed content for the moment, basking in my attention. She looked over her shoulder and stared down the hill to where Skoki was standing. He was minding his own business by the pond near the front of the enclosure, with his back turned to Khutzy. She turned back toward me. I noticed a wee smile on her face, and for a fleeting moment I thought we were making progress. Wrong again!

Next in her protracted fit of jealousy, Khutzy spun around and flung herself down the hill, barely touching down, jetting across the water like an angry stone, headed for Skoki. There was no huffing, no warning, as she launched herself onto Skoki's back from the rear and bit into the muscled hump behind his neck. Skoki roared, bucked forward, and swung from side to side to shake her off. Louise, trying to save her offensive "cub" from Skoki's self-defense tactics, confronted Skoki head-on, yelling and spitting only a snout's length from his face. Outnumbered, Skoki sank his giant canines into Louise's upper jaw, ripping open her lip and creating a deep gash in her nose. I added to the deafening growls screaming my dictum, "No fights! No fights!" as I flew down the long staircase on the hill to get to the front of the enclosure. This was a zookeeper's nightmare. Finally, at the front, I spun around to the only zoo visitor there and demanded, "Who won?" The bears had split, and my view of the end of the battle had been blocked by shrubbery lining the staircase. All three bears were suddenly quiet. As Louise came up to the fence to show me her bleeding wounds, the man said, "You did!"

It is important to be responsive to bears when they solicit your assistance. Open mouthed, Louise hung her head forward to demonstrate the flowing blood, which had stopped streaming and was now only dripping, like tears, onto the ground. She looked like the prize fighter she was. Her upper lip was cut open right to the base of her nose and she had a large hole where Skoki's upper canine had pierced her sinuses. That had to hurt. I said, "Louise, courtyard." She needed to see a doctor for her wounds. This meant that I had to get her into a confined area like the courtyard in case our veterinarian decided that we needed to anesthetize her to sew up her face.

Louise and I parted ways at the front of the enclosure. She climbed the hill in the enclosure, went through the mesh tunnel, and turned to her right out into the courtyard. I climbed the staircase behind the shrubbery, went in through the bear building's back door, grabbed a brick of ice cream and a wooden spoon, went out the building's front door, headed east around the south side of the courtyard, through the gate, and around to the north fence, where Louise was waiting for me. Louise clearly knew what the word "courtyard" meant, since she showed up there before I did. I radioed for the veterinary staff to come. Louise communicated her pain with a single, gentle bite to her raised paw as she stared at me. That demonstration alone must have hurt, since she was doing it with a split lip. As we waited, I closed the bear gates, not so much to keep Louise in as to keep Skoki and

Khutzy out. Remarkably, Skoki and Khutzy, who had been in the depths of fierce battle not twenty minutes earlier, were now standing quietly, side by side, at the north fence of the large enclosure and staring across the way at Louise and the ice cream.

Our vet arrived, and I gave Louise a few wooden spoonfuls of vanilla ice cream—her favorite—to entice her to come over and let us look at her wounds up close. The ice cream also cooled off the injured area, helping with the inevitable pain, and rewarded her for coming up to the courtyard when I asked her to. The fact that she could tolerate the ice cream around her mouth was a good sign. Our veterinarian decided not to bother stitching up Louise's lip, since Louise would likely rip out the stitches, and prescribed a dose of antibiotics and painkillers over the next ten days. Roughly translated, this meant one drug-laced ice cream slurry twice a day for Louise.

There were no more rip-roaring group fights after this round. Perhaps the bears had settled the issue that day, or perhaps Louise was now in estrus—full-blown heat. Grizzly bear females, like females of other bear species, are thought to be induced ovulators.[3] This is part of nature's energy conservation strategy. If you live most of your adult life independent of other adults in your species, then it makes sense to only spend energy on releasing eggs and developing hormones and other juices that allow you to warm up to the opposite sex when males are actually around. Otherwise, why bother?

Before Skoki arrived and Louise lived with just the girls (Khutzy and Florence), she spent a great deal of time in the spring meticulously rubbing her hind quarters onto rocks and logs. These were scent signals designed to attract one or many mates. From Louise's perspective one might say it worked. Skoki showed up and—fancy that—he arrived at breeding time! Like the males, grizzly bear females are promiscuous. But male grizzly bears have been known to kill off the yearling cubs of a female, presumably so that she will stop producing milk, go back into estrus, breed with him, and pass on his genes. This is counterproductive for a mother, who spends, on average, two and a half years raising her cubs before they are ready to go out on their own. It may be that females have adapted by breeding with all of the local boys to trick them into believing that the cubs they see her with the following year belong to each of them. This would keep the males from killing her cubs, and they will move on to the next viable female.[4]

Louise and Skoki had successfully carried out the dance steps that their genetics required of them to mate. Now they were coupled in heat, exclusively focused on each other. I had not fully appreciated just how fixated breeding bear pairs could be until I watched the so-utterly ignored Khutzy run interference.

While Skoki and Louise were coupled—which was all of the time, with rare intermissions—Khutzy approached them and rested her head on the back of Louise's neck. When that failed to draw attention, she went behind the couple and tried to rest her head on Skoki's rump. This didn't work, because Skoki was standing on two legs and resting his torso on Louise's back, and Khutzy's head kept sliding off. Khutzy wandered circles around the pair, looking and sticking her nose in places where it clearly didn't belong, seemingly trying to unlock the secret to membership in this club.

On one occasion, Khutzy lay down, rolled over onto her back perpendicular to the breeding pair, and attempted to wiggle under the standing Louise. This caused the bear pyramid to fall apart on top of Khutzy, only to be rebuilt farther away without her. Several times, Khutzy hurriedly walked up to me at the fence, looked me in the eyes, and demonstrated with a single gentle bite into a lifted paw while looking in the direction of the couple. She was in pain—being ignored for the first time in your life hurts. Before I could give her some much-sought attention, she was gone again, back over to study the couple.

Without understanding the consequences, Khutzy finally managed to unscramble the Rubik's Cube. She sidled up to Louise and carefully mimicked her breeding stance, taking note of where and how each of Louise's feet were positioned and how her head was held. *This* got Skoki's attention! He slid off Louise's back and was now staring at two female rumps in breeding position. When bears are exceptionally contented and at ease, they often have what can only be described as a goofy look on their faces. Their eyelids droop, and the mouth is slightly open, the lower lip hanging loose, forming a little trough—sometimes catching drool—while the upper lip is smiling. Skoki had this expression on his face. *Two* female rumps in breeding position! Skoki sidestepped to the left and mounted Khutzy from behind. She bolted forward, whirled around, faced Skoki, jaws snapping and spit flying, and then galloped off. The goofy expression never left Skoki's face as he remounted Louise and resumed his business. Khutzy left the couple alone and spent the rest of the day in and around the pond.

After this, there was a subtle change in the air. While still maintaining friendly, nonaggressive relations with Skoki, Louise grew less interested in coupling. Undaunted, Skoki spent his now free time pursuing Khutzy. He was much less aggressive with Khutzy than he had been with Louise and kept his distance when

Khutzy tired of his following behavior and flew at him with an open mouth, baring her canines, demonstrating her biting-his-face technique in the air. Perhaps he understood her lack of experience or just didn't want to incite another riot or both.

For the first time in her life, Khutzy cycled and bred, even though it was now fall. Skoki was twice her size, and she practically disappeared when they coupled. Skoki couldn't just relax and hang his torso off of Khutzy's back during intromission as he did with Louise. He had to get off of Khutzy, because she couldn't handle his weight for very long, and when her strength gave out, she simply sat down, putting an end to the session. They were both young bears and found other ways to hang together.

Skoki would sit and Khutzy would stand on her hind legs while they fenced, open mouthed. Once I observed Khutzy stick her head—up to her forehead—into Skoki's giant mouth. They repeated this behavior over and over; smiling between throat-dives. While I interpreted this as play, it also served to bond the two animals of vastly different sizes. Khutzy demonstrated that she was not afraid of Skoki, and Skoki demonstrated that he would not be aggressive with her. If anything, Skoki had proven time and again his enormous patience with this little diva bear. Louise was not left out, as she joined Khutzy and Skoki during rest periods, and all three bears slept together in a bear pile. Breeding served this group well, as it had allowed the bears to get to know each other and cemented their relationship.

As breeding behaviors waned, Louise and Khutzy resumed their relationship as mother and cub. Fall had arrived, and, as is typical for Calgary, all of the leaves fell off the trees in two days. The temperatures alternated between cold and warm, and once in a while we would still have a hot day. The three bears were ravenous all of the time and divided their time between eating everything we gave them and choosing their winter den. Skoki claimed squatter's rights to a den site first; he chose the den that other bears had dug before him in the hill in the outside enclosure. This wasn't surprising, since Skoki had spent the previous winter outside in the wild. The girls—who also preferred the outside den—decided to den together in the building den room.

I have spent hundreds of hours of my life watching bears prepare their nesting sites. Each nest is a fascinating reflection of who each bear is as an individual. The nest architecture, functionality, and orderliness are personal. Skoki—like many male bears—had a bulldozer approach to nest building. His den had a short entrance tunnel about three feet long, which had water-pooling problems, and a room off to the left as you entered which was about one cubic yard. It was too small for Skoki's fall girth and needed work. But I wasn't ready for his renovation plan. When he wasn't eating, he was digging. Initially, we could see his rump sticking out of the entrance as he dug, flinging fresh earth out of the den and trickling down the slope of the hill. He eventually disappeared into the den as he excavated. Over time we got a little concerned, as the expelled soil grew into a substantial pile beneath the den entrance. I crawled in to make inspections whenever I could, to be certain he wasn't digging his way out of the enclosure. It smelled pungent, like wet bear. Skoki had added a second room to the right. It was about one and a half cubic yards—large enough to handle Skoki's seasonally expanded girth.

One weekend I came down with a cold. I was mouth-breathing because my sinuses were so clogged, my eyes were runny and crusty, and I was drop-dead tired. When I returned to work, I noticed that construction on the outside den had ceased. I assumed that the job was done. Usually Skoki and the girls came up to greet me when I arrived in the morning. That day, Louise and Khutzy came, but not Skoki. I searched the large enclosure for him but couldn't find him. When I went into the building, I found Skoki lying on his side in a straw nest in the inner bedroom. This was unusual, since he didn't like to spend time indoors. He raised his head slightly and looked at me. He looked like me! He was mouth-breathing, had runny, crusty eyes with droopy eyelids, and looked drop-dead tired. I called one of the veterinarians, who came and diagnosed both Skoki and me with head colds. Our vet said he had never seen a bear with a cold before, but that was definitely what it appeared to be. We would go with that diagnosis unless Skoki's symptoms persisted. Until then, there wasn't much the vet could do to help either of us except to tell us both to keep a low profile for the rest of the day. I felt responsible, since I figured I had unwittingly given Skoki my cold.

I was finally able to clear my sinuses by taking several spoonfuls of Buckley's Mixture cough syrup. It tasted like turpentine, however, and I knew there was no way I would be able to get this medicine into Skoki.

I decided to try Halls Mentho-Lyptus cough drops with a liquid centre. The goo center was important. Skoki was more discerning about processed human foods than Louise or Khutzy. For instance, he wouldn't eat Fruit Loops breakfast cereal as a training reward. Skoki didn't recognize it as a food, never mind a treat, and after biting into it to test it, he would spit it out. I was certain that he would not like the Mentho-Lyptus taste, but this combination was the only other way I could think of to clear his sinuses.

With the goo center, I reasoned, he would have some of it still stuck in his mouth when he tried to spit out the hard candy.

It was imperative that he bite into the candy before chucking it. When I needed to get a new concept across to a bear, it was sometimes useful to demonstrate, like a human mother who demonstrates the edibility of carrots to her five-year-old offspring by eating some herself. So I sat, open mouthed, by the fence with Skoki and dramatically placed a Halls cough drop on my tongue, brought it into my mouth, and loudly crunched it, then moved my mouth around as if to eat it. Skoki appeared expressionless and unenthusiastic about the lesson, but he stayed with me. So I repeated the show and concluded by holding out a Halls for him. Keeping his eyes glued to mine, he apprehensively took the candy with his lips, brought it back into his mouth, and crunched it with his molars. Immediately he jerked upward as if to try to escape the taste, fumbled with his tongue to find the tiny pieces, and attempted to spit them out. But they stuck to his tongue and lips, and there was no expelling the goo. He stared back at me in disgust. Then he stopped, appearing to notice a difference, broke his stare, and breathed in very slightly through his nose, as if he were feeling the menthol-eucalyptus at work opening up his nasal passages. I reasoned that it would take a lot more than one Halls to clear his massive sinuses, so I continued to hand them to him as long as he wanted them. He took another one and crunched it, then another and another. He had dozens of them. Periodically he would attempt to breathe deeply and fully through his nose. When his nose breathing became constant, he stopped taking them.

His mood seemed to lighten as he huffed and shook his head back and forth in an obvious attempt to clear his sinuses. I was still sitting close by him at the fence. Suddenly he froze, turned toward me, extended his face, mouth open, and sneezed. Out came an ocean spray of slime and gunk, which landed on my glasses, face, hair, and coat. Skoki was smiling. I guessed the treatment had been successful.

The concept of using something to alleviate a physical discomfort would not have been new to Skoki.[5] Bears seem to seek such relief by trial and error or are taught what to do by their mothers. Skoki resumed his den reconstruction the next day.

Louise and Khutzy were also preparing their winter den, although, as is typical of mother bears, Louise was doing most of the work. She spent hours raking small piles of leaves and sticks toward herself with her claws, continuously backing up the hill and into the den room in the building. Khutzy would start a pile outside and then run off to investigate something else. Squirrels—also looking for nest-building material—would generally come along and rob her unguarded pile, so she always seemed to be starting over again. I assisted by dropping off two bales of straw in the inner bedroom for Louise to fluff and maneuver however she chose and two bales outside for Skoki. The next morning, I noticed that Louise had taken all of the straw from the bedroom into the den room and puffed it so that it was at least three feet deep. As I surveyed her overnight work, Louise came through the door, rump first, raking a huge pile of straw from Skoki's cache outside. How would I secure enough straw for Skoki if Louise stole it all?

As the fall chill turned into winter's cold, the straw problem turned out not to be an issue. Skoki had lined his den with leaves and sticks. His nest was not elaborate like the girls' nest, but the new wing that he had added was impressive. That week, the temperature dropped from sixty degrees Fahrenheit to minus forty, where Fahrenheit meets Celsius, and the grizzly bears disappeared.[6] I could check on the girls in their den by quietly lifting the flap of a small peephole in the keeper area. I had no way of checking on Skoki in his outside den and had to assume that he was there and all right. He had overwintered the previous ten years without my help, I reasoned, so he was likely fine now. Over the next ten weeks, the snow fell until it was up to my knees.

Skoki was never far from my thoughts. I couldn't help but wonder what it would feel like for Skoki to wake after a winter of denning and remember that he was not in the Skoki Valley but in an enclosure with Louise and Khutzy. Did he think like that? He had not been with us for more than a few months before it was time to hibernate. Would there be a few moments after he woke—before he came out of his den—when he would have forgotten? Would it wash over him like a grim reality as it does for a traumatized human who finds a reprieve in sleep, just forgets for a moment on waking, and then remembers? I didn't know. I was concerned that he might regress in his acclimation to captivity, which could mean a change in his behavior.

Finally, a Chinook wind warmed up the Bow Valley and Calgary with it. It was now January. I was checking the fence line of the large enclosure and coming up the hill on the wooden staircase, enjoying the blue Alberta sky and the brilliant sunlight bouncing off the snow. Skoki stuck his head out of the den entrance. I thought I would sit by the fence and quietly watch while he got his bearings. But my two-way radio went off and gave me away. Skoki turned and saw me. He came out of the den and galloped over to visit, smiling. I was quite surprised.

CHAPTER 4

A PACING POLAR BEAR

Snowball's Inner Demon

EVERY EXTRA MINUTE I had, I would stand in front of the old polar bear exhibit at the Calgary Zoo. I would watch and wonder as the three adult female polar bears, Candy, Misty, and Snowball, paced in tandem, each on her own path, back and forth. It was mesmerizing and seriously disturbing. As a novice keeper in the mid-1980s, I asked more experienced zookeepers why. Why did three otherwise healthy animals pace seemingly constantly? I was told not to worry; polar bears walk great distances in the wild, and when they are brought into captivity, they pace.

That made no sense to me. Pacing looked nothing like the purposeful and directional lumbering of a wild polar bear. It didn't even look like Candy, Misty, and Snowball's normal walk to and from specific locations. The pacing gait was regimented—so many steps in one direction, the same number of steps back—feet falling in exactly the same locations as before. Who walks like that? The turn to go back often included elaborate head swings in figure eights or half moons, and repetitive jaw snapping and huffing at precisely the same time in the routine on every repetition. From a few telephone calls to friends working in other zoos, I found out that we were lucky because our bears paced in what appeared to be a fairly normal way. Some bears in other zoos paced backward, swam in circles, swung their heads back and forth, sometimes against walls, or rubbed themselves raw on rocks. Clearly our "walking great distances in the wild" theory fell apart under the weight of these absurdly incongruous behaviors.

Taking one last stab at that theory, I reasoned that a bear who had been born in the wild and had some experience living there might have a stronger urge to express distance walking in captivity—a sort of nature-plus-nurture advantage. Misty, who was born in northern Manitoba to a wild mother, was adopted as a yearling orphan cub by Candy, the wild-born mother of captive-born Snowball at the Calgary Zoo. Of the three females, it was captive-born Snowball who seemed to spend most of her day locked into this pacing pattern. Misty would not pace for months at a time, and Candy showed varying degrees of daily down time.

Polar bears are not automatons that repetitiously reproduce a behavior just because they are genetically encoded with the ability to express that behavior—like walking great distances in the wild to find food and mates. Bears are opportunistic and able to respond to their immediate circumstances, so the presence of readily available food and mates in captivity overrides their need to travel and makes walking great distances a useless and wasteful expenditure of energy. That seemed to be the obvious problem. Like animals in most other zoos, Candy,

Misty, and Snowball lived in a barren, cement environment devoid of variation and new stimuli. Their husbandry routine was equally barren. They were cleaned at the same time and fed the same food, at the same time, in the same location, every day, year after year. Perhaps they were responding to their immediate circumstances.

Their home was a thousand-square-yard cement fortress with walls that were twenty-five feet high and one three feet thick, painted sea-ice blue on the inside. The exhibit was encased by ground-floor viewing windows on two sides, and there was rooftop viewing into the bear pit on three sides. The pit itself—which was about nine hundred square yards—housed a square, forty-five-thousand-gallon cement pool that was about ten feet deep. The floor of the back of the exhibit crested at about thirteen feet higher than the front of the exhibit. This change in height accommodated the flow of a waterfall from the back wall into the large pool, and the water then cascaded into a smaller, shallow, crescent-moon-shaped pool (full of pebbles) less than three feet deep. Bill Dubreuil, an animal care foreman at that time, referred to it as "early seventies, impressionistic ice-floe" architecture. This exhibit was like a permanent, unchanging snapshot, presumably built to look like springtime in the Arctic—the only time of the year when there actually could be a flowing waterfall, however ephemeral it might be.

Cement is the operative word here—cement, cement, and more cement. The enclosure was purposely cement and purposely barren. To understand why any human would do such a thing to a polar bear, who is today commonly understood to be a fully sentient being, one has to go back into the thinking of the time. It is unwise to judge yesterday's thinking by today's standards, but it is critical to understand the thoughts that propelled us into today. We are responsible for doing better when we know better.

In 1576, Marty Frobisher explored Frobisher Bay in Arctic Canada. Bill Baffin explored Hudson Strait and Baffin Bay in 1615 and 1616. In 1728, Vit Bering found the Bering Strait, and so on. The act of exploring the grossly inhospitable Arctic proved to be extremely dangerous to the nonnative naked ape and was, in those days, akin to modern-day space exploration. In the soup of told and regurgitated exploration adventure stories, including disputed land claims, get-rich-quick schemes, and horrific deaths from malnutrition and incurable diseases, one indisputable truth always rose to the top of every telling: polar bears are extremely dangerous, and if you kill them, your status among men and women greatly improves. In the absence of other meaningful natural history information to help balance the human perspective, this overemphasis on a polar bear's predatory qualities has done more to hurt the animal than any other single factor in history, with the exception of global warming today.

The blastoff of Sputnik 1 in October 1957 launched the space age, which yielded lightweight, hardy materials that were spun into clothing and forged into tools to allow us to visit space, as well as inhospitable earthly environments, with greater ease. The Arctic was opened up to not just brave information-seeking scientists and naturalists but also to anyone with the money and lust to overcome the deadly polar bear, using high-powered rifles, clothing compliments of NASA, mechanized sleds, and sometimes cruise ships.[1] Indiscriminate global hunting practices brought polar bears to their knees in the mid-1960s.

A 1965 meeting of scientists from the five countries that polar bears are indigenous to—Canada, the United States, the then Soviet Union, Norway, and Denmark—led to a historically significant and scientifically sound polar bear conservation agreement between these countries, and it was ratified in Oslo in 1976. The international Agreement on the Conservation of Polar Bears and their habitat, known to wildlife researchers as the Oslo Agreement,[2] is historically significant because it is the one thing Arctic countries have been able to agree on. It is ironic that, in August 2007, the Russians planted a flag on the ocean floor under the globally warmed and rapidly receding North Pole ice cap—home of the polar bear—to lay claim to the rest of the Lomonosov Ridge, leaving Canadians and Americans scrambling for icebreakers to deal with this transgression. The Oslo Agreement is not based on politics and is scientifically thorough, as it defines practical conservation procedures including hunting moratoriums, the setting of native hunting quotas, habitat preservation, and shared research efforts.[3]

So what does all of this have to do with the building of cement fortresses to house polar bears in zoos? We built them because we were afraid of polar bears, and we knew little about them. The Oslo Agreement did for polar bears what Jane Goodall did for chimpanzees[4] and Dian Fossey did for gorillas:[5] it generated wildlife research. To care for animals properly, you have to know about their living requirements. Every bit of information about polar bears' lives in the wild, to which they are genetically adapted, was devoured by those zookeepers who were looking for answers. Seemingly ad hoc research projects, each identifying and dissertating a pixel of the polar bear's life in the wild, helped to create a whole picture that zookeepers could use to identify what was missing back in the cement pit. A cumulative, authoritative work by Ian Stirling, aptly titled *Polar Bears*,[6] emerged and became a guide to a polar bear's needs for me and many others.

Not only were we afraid *of* them, we were also afraid *for* them, which is why we housed them in barren exhibits. This is going to be difficult to explain. Not only is it the thinking of several generations before me, but it flies in the face of everything I believe in, which is a holistic approach to life. How we care for our animals is a reflection of our cultural beliefs.

I can remember reading a short entry in the zookeeper's daily polar bear husbandry journal from the early 1980s describing how Snowball had ripped a wooden board from one of the sleeping platforms in the building. She had brought the plank into the outside enclosure and was playing with it. Candy and Misty were involved too, taking turns manipulating, licking, and gnawing on the plank. The plank was retrieved within forty-eight hours. I know the keeper, and he worried himself sick the whole time wondering if the bears would try to eat the plank, get splinters in their paws or noses, rip out their teeth, or surf the plank right through the pool window into the public viewing area—which would be very bad. The keeper took it away from the bears for the same reason he would have taken the plank away from a five-year-old child: because she might get hurt.

In the 1950s and '60s, humans had declared warfare against bacteria—and sometimes bacterial warfare against each other. Again, without other information to balance the perspective, humans reasoned that all—well, most—bacteria were bad, and if we eradicated them we would be healthy and could avoid diseases and survive surgeries. Not that this was wrong—it was just extreme. As a result, health was viewed as meaning germ-free. In a preemptive strike, we built living spaces with space-age smooth surfaces that could be thoroughly disinfected. Homes, hospitals, public places, and zoos were lined with tiles and sealed cement. Bears in cement grottos and gorillas in tiled cages were subject to mechanistic cleaning protocols that interfered with the animals' individual needs to identify territory, good food sources, and so on by scent.

We fastidiously focused on germs. If, as a captive animal, your sense of well-being depended on a personally scent-marked home space or you received your information about the mood of your cagemates by smelling their droppings, you were simply out of luck, since every day all of your information sources were literally washed down the drain. Natural objects like trees, logs, boulders, and pebbles were difficult to clean. Animals made a mess and could get hurt if they interacted with these objects, so we simply didn't include them in the animals' enclosures.

Not everyone was so ritualistically fixated on disinfection. Heini Hediger, a Swiss ethology professor generally given credit for the birth of zoo biology, spoke and wrote about the primal importance of enriching animals' lives by offering choice in complex captive-living environments.[7] He was ahead of his time, as we continued to build flashy, uniform, easily disinfected rows of barren cages and grottoes. The problem wasn't with Hediger's thinking but with its appeal to the public.

After the Second World War, we focused on technology— we wanted off the planet and into the stars. *Natural* wasn't in; it wasn't sciencey or space-agey enough. So cement grottos and tiled cages dotted the global zoo landscape. Because of the direction science was taking, animals were housed in a dirt-free environment. By the time we understood that animals could not conform to life in barren, cement enclosures, a new generation of zoo professionals had inherited these monstrosities and the seriously understimulated animals that inhabited them. It can take several human generations to work popular notions—no matter how bizarre and obviously unfit those notions are—out of mainstream culture.

At the Calgary Zoo, I was fortunate to work with managers such as Peter Karsten, the zoo's director, and Greg Tarry, the then director of animal care, who grieved the limitations of barren, cement enclosures and had begun a zoo-wide master plan to replace them with complex, natural enclosures. Polar bears and all of the other animals who lived in barren, cement enclosures were in the master plan to receive new, natural digs, but the list was long, and it would take time and money to get to every animal in need. In the interim, anyone who showed an interest in improving the well-being of any animal was supported. Snowball's incessant pacing beckoned to me every day.

Snowball was born in November of 1969 in one of the old, barred cages in the cat-and-bear string, which had also housed Louise when she first arrived at the Calgary Zoo. Candy, Snowball's mother, was a wild-born captive female who had been purchased from settlers somewhere in the Hudson Bay area in 1965 at the age of one. She was likely orphaned by hunters, but the records are sketchy. Having been brought up by her natal mother, Candy understood how to rear her own cubs. She gave birth to two cubs in the den attached to the small barred exhibit. Keeper staff monitored her around the clock and tended to her needs with straw and food, should she want to eat.

Three weeks after the keepers first heard a cub's cry in the den, they spotted a fluffy, fully furred cub at the door. Single cub sightings continued for another two weeks until one keeper spotted two cubs, one significantly larger than the other. Two weeks later, the keepers saw the smaller cub lying in the doorway, dead. The remaining cub—Snowball—was active and strong and followed her mother on excursions out of the den ten weeks after first being heard. Four months later, in May, Snowball's mother enticed her over to the little cement pool and taught her to swim.

Snowball was first recorded pacing at the age of two and a half, when she was moved into her own enclosure, away from Candy and a male cagemate. Veterinarians tried to calm her with a tranquilizer, but it failed to help her. Snowball was returned to her old cage with Candy and the male, and her pacing stopped. Snowball resumed her pacing behavior in earnest when all of the polar bears—there were five in total—were moved to their new, impressionistic ice-floe exhibit in the fall of 1973. The oral history of Snowball, as told by now retired zookeepers, indicates that she began to pace because she was afraid of various aggressive males with whom she had to live—and one in particular, named Carmichael II, who was thought to have drowned several female bears—when she was younger. Eventually, Snowball's pacing became a habit that she had engaged in for twenty-two years, long after the last male died.

Regardless of the history of the pacing habit, Snowball's enclosure needed greater complexity. Polar bears are known for their ingenuity in hunting prey. Biologists have described a motionless, floating-bear "ice floe" with the bear's backside above the waterline and her head submerged. When a seal comes within striking distance, the ice floe comes horribly to life.[8] Any animal who is genetically endowed to think of such a complex and creative food-gathering strategy needs more from her environment than cement and a pyramid pile of processed omnivore chow once a day.

I started to work on this problem in the summer of 1992. Candy had died of lung cancer in 1990 at the age of 26, leaving Snowball and Misty. It was extraordinarily difficult to get to know these bears, because of the impenetrable cement walls and thick windows. The only place where I could be with them face-to-face was in the back area of the building, where the bear bedrooms were. It included a row of small, cement rooms joined at the rear by a bear access hall and at the front by a keeper access hall. Although there was lighting, it always seemed dark and dank. Snowball was more forward than Misty and would allow me to work with her in the back. Misty was always very skittish back there—fearful that she might be locked inside, since that happened regularly to accommodate the cleaning of the outdoor exhibit. She typically stood in the back bear doorway so that she could make a quick escape should she need to. Misty let Snowball work with the humans and do most things first. This was likely a behavior that had developed when they were younger— Snowball knew the neighborhood and Misty didn't.

Misty was a wild-born female yearling cub who arrived at the Calgary Zoo in 1976, when Snowball was seven years old. Candy, Snowball's mother, adopted Misty and raised them both as siblings. It made sense that Misty would acquiesce to Snowball's knowledge of captive living and learn from it. Their lives were relatively unchanging in the cement pit, so there was no need for Misty and Snowball to modify this arrangement.

This suited me fine for now, since it was Snowball's pacing that I hoped to help first. Foremost, we needed to bond. I began by hand-feeding Snowball some grapes through the bars at the keeper gate. It took a few weeks before Snowball would come up to me. As I bonded with Snowball, I also tossed grapes back to Misty, who was standing in the back bear doorway. Separating the two so that I could work exclusively with Snowball was not an option. These two bears did everything together. Snowball would not interact with me if I separated her from Misty.

It was difficult enough trying to find the time to work with Snowball, because she always seemed to be pacing. I had a heck of a time trying to convince her to stop for long enough to have a bonding session. Often I'd have to catch her between pacing sessions.

If a bear or any animal—including a human—has lived in a barren environment for years with little to no change, you have to ease her into the concept of change so that you don't scare her. The one item that the polar bears did have was a big blue plastic barrel that always resided in the pool. I started making change by dragging the drum into the back area and simply standing it upright on the floor in the room adjacent to the back bear door. Snowball and Misty had heard the ruckus and stood on the outside of the closed door. When I opened it to let them in, they just stood there, side-by-side in the doorway, motionless for a full thirty seconds, staring at the barrel and then, moving their eyeballs only, staring at me. I stood there with my pad and pencil ready to make notes on their behavior. Snowball snapped to, lunged forward, and smacked the barrel with her front right paw, sending it crashing against the bars in front of me as she exhaled with a rush of air that sounded like a mighty steam engine, registering her complaint. Misty exploded out of the doorway into the exhibit and Snowball followed. I stood there with my pad and pencil. ok then—that was our first enrichment event!

Every day, I moved the barrel to a different location. As the days passed, the bears grew accustomed to my odd behavior and learned to retrieve the barrel from wherever it was and chuck it back into the pool to play with. At the same time, I made friends with them by bribing them with scatter feeds of foods they either had never seen before or had not seen for a long time. Because it was summer and I did not want them to consume unnecessary calories, I took advantage of their natural behavior and gave them vegetable matter like melons, berries, and other fruits, and tubers like yams.

One of the problems for bears in captivity is obesity accompanied by inactivity. This may seem like an odd thing to say about polar bears, since weight loss and weight gain are a normal part of their annual cycle. But obesity is a problem for a polar bear when she does not have enough lean body mass (muscle) to hang her fat off of. If, when the bear stands up on her hind legs, her body fat drops down and hangs like liquid in a plastic bag around her hips, giving her a pear shape, then she is obese and under-muscled. The "pear bear" phenomenon is quite common in captive polar bears, who are given the same diet throughout the year, regardless of the season or their ability to be active.

Polar bears that live far enough south to experience seasonality in the wild have to put on great amounts of body fat and accompanying muscle in the spring and early summer, before the ice has receded, to get them through their summer fasting—or walking hibernation, as it is often referred to. Even more critically, expectant mothers also have to get through the subsequent winter's birthing and nursing on what they have stored up from the previous spring. Polar bears do this by hunting fat-rich, newly weaned spring seal pups while there is still pack ice.[9] Wild polar bears can gain hundreds of pounds of fat and not become "pear bears" because they are active and generate lots of muscle mass.

To provide enrichment events for Snowball and Misty in the warm Calgary summer months, I took advantage of the fact that wild polar bears that are landlocked will eat bog blueber-ries, black crowberry, and other tundra vegetation.[10] This means that, despite their famed preference for seal fat, polar bears are in fact seasonally omnivorous and can eat both animal and plant matter.

With our veterinarians' blessings, we added a large variety of berries, fruits, and seeds to the scatter feeds, including raspber-ries, strawberries, blueberries, gooseberries, cherries, tomatoes, plums, and peaches. We also included raisins, peanuts, sun-flower seeds, and mealworms—not that they are berries, but they were a big hit. During the scatter feeds, Misty would meticulously search until the last seed had been hunted down. Snowball rooted for foods for a while—sometimes for longer periods of time, sometimes shorter—depending on how desir-able the foods were. Then she would go back to pacing. At least she spent more time on berries, peanuts, and mealworms.

During one enrichment event, I scattered hundreds of live crickets throughout the enclosure. Snowball and Misty were anxiously excited and ran around chasing bugs until one cricket accidentally jumped into Snowball's substantial nostril. She leapt backward, shook her head, and sneezed and woofed long after the cricket had been blasted out of her nose. Snowball was com-pletely put off, ceased her cricket hunt, and went back to pacing.

On another occasion, the zoo had received a donation of half a dozen five-gallon buckets filled to the brim with slightly sour blackberries. None of the other animals would eat them, so I mashed them into a compote with sugar and water and froze them solid in the buckets. The next afternoon, I hauled all six blackberrysicles up to the upper deck of the polar bear building and dropped them like bombs into the pool. Snowball immediately dove in, tucked one under each arm, and paddled back to shore using her hind legs. Misty had no intention of jumping into the pool to get one. She just hung over the edge and popped one out from under Snowball's arm before Snowball could get on shore, and ran off with it. I watched their behaviors for a short while, just to make sure that each got at least one berrysicle before it melted away in the pool.

While attending a meeting in the education building, I received a cryptically panicked call on the two-way radio from security. Would I come to the polar bear building immediately?! Being asked to come back *immediately* to your building was never good, and I imagined everything from a possible escape to a *possible escape*! I ran back down to the polar bear building and met the security officer outside. He grabbed my arm, pulled me aside, and hissed—he was very stressed—that the polar bears were blood-red around their mouths and front paws, and so was the entire pool. I was very stressed. Forgetting about the blackberrysicles, I raced to the pool as fast as my cement-heavy legs could carry me. At the pool viewing window, the sight was incredible—the pool was an eerie, watery red and had what seemed like millions of minuscule blackberry seeds suspended in it. I spent the rest of the afternoon explaining blackberrysicles and the merits of enrichment events for bears to zoo visitors. Snowball had gone back to her pacing, and Misty had gone for a nap. But they were both quite formidable looking with their white fur stained red.

Normally, I didn't have buckets of bloody berries, so I made fishsicles or squidsicles. Snowball would dive in after them and tuck one under each arm. Misty would wait on deck to steal one from her before Snowball could get out of the pool. Interestingly, she never fought with Misty over these treats. They fought so rarely that the only episode I can clearly remember seemed to be over a raisin that they were both reaching for at the same time. Snowball had a broad head with a Roman nose—a feature sometimes attributed to male polar bears. It was a no-nonsense polar bear face, whereas Misty was beautiful by human standards. She had a long, slender nose, with a furless freckle just below her right eye. Her brows protruded slightly, adding expression to her face. Arguing over raisin rights, both bears looked seriously ferocious as they fenced with open mouths and growled, their fur standing on end. At one point Snowball engulfed Misty's upper jaw in her mouth, but neither bear bit the other.

For one event, I bought two huge, whole watermelons for the bears. As with the ice treats, I dropped them into the pool from the upper deck. Each melon caused a geyserlike splash and a small tidal wave as the water fully swallowed it and then spit it up to float on the surface. Snowball dove in immediately. Misty ran to wait by the pool's edge. But Snowball had trouble. She tried to tuck the first melon under her arm, but it shot out from under her. She swam over to retrieve the other melon. This time, she was able to keep it under her arm but couldn't swim. It buoyed up her right side and rolled her over in the water. With a pointy upper lip and some jaw snapping and huffing, Snowball told the watermelon off. The melon didn't seem to care, how-ever, and shot out from under her too. Misty was drooling and tap dancing with her front paws, swinging impatiently back and forth on deck. Snowball went after the first melon again and pushed it ahead of her over toward the second watermelon. She mounted one melon under her right arm and one under her left arm. Now she was completely buoyed up by melons—almost upright—and attempted to paddle back to shore using her rear paws. It was like watching a five-year-old child wearing water wings—not conducive to actual swimming.

Snowball's trip back to shore went slowly, sometimes in pirouettes. Eventually she made it. She was very tired. Misty punted one melon out from under Snowball's arm to grab it, but it shot back out to sea. Snowball ignored it and got out of the pool with *her* melon. Misty looked at Snowball, and Snowball lowered her head and stared back at Misty. It was clear that Snowball had no intention of giving up this watermelon. Misty dove into the pool and moved the melon to shore in front of her. The retrieval of the watermelons took so much problem-solving skill that I repeated it often.

The bears had gotten used to items being in their enclosure and being moved around. I wanted to up the ante by developing enrichment events that would challenge their thinking. The polar bear enclosure contained a barred room that historically had been used as a feeding area. I had stopped feeding the bears there and now changed the location and timing of feedings daily except for breakfast. I had noticed that having breakfast as soon as possible in the morning was vital to the bears, or they would start to pace in anticipation of or impatience for food. By the time I arrived at work at seven AM, the bears had already been up since four or five, and they were hungry. If I fed them immediately, that could put off the pacing for a while longer that day.

I built a tall barricade of plastic barrels and logs between the feeding room and the back bear door into the building. Then I placed herring and trout on the floor of the feeding room, which Snowball and Misty could see from the exhibit, as incentive to take down the barricade. To get into the feeding room, the bears had to go through the building. When I opened the back bear door, Snowball and Misty stood there motionless, each staring at the barricade, and then, moving their eyeballs only, they stared at me. We seemed to have gone back to the day that I first moved their barrel into the back. Remarkably, Misty was the first to step forward, and attempted to move a log near the bottom of the pile. The pile adjusted itself, and a plastic barrel fell down and bounced off her head. I felt a little sorry for her. With a pointy upper lip, she told the log and me off by huffing and doing some slight jaw-snapping and forward head swinging as she stepped back. Snowball moved up and began to dismantle the barricade from the top. When the path to the herring and trout was open, Misty ran in and ate the fish. Snowball walked outside and resumed her pacing.

One of the most ingenious problem-solving sessions I observed came during an enrichment event when I dropped the barrel into the exhibit from the upper deck. It was closed at both ends, except for two four-inch holes on one end, opposite each other, near the rim. I had placed a dozen herring in the barrel through the holes. Snowball immediately broke her pace and got to the barrel first. Misty got up from her nap and came over to watch. Snowball manipulated the barrel every which way she could think of so that the fish would drop out. It didn't happen. Then she pawed at the holes, but her giant, furry, clawed fingers could not get in far enough. Snowball dragged the barrel into the pool and repeated the investigative behaviors she had used on land, turning the barrel every which way. Water had started to enter the barrel through one submerged hole. Snowball stuck her eyeball into the other hole, peering in at the herring. She then purposefully pushed the barrel halfway below the water line. As the barrel filled up with water that had come through the bottom hole, it eventually came gushing out of the top hole, and the fish came rushing out with the water. Misty dove into the water to share in the bounty. One fish remained in the barrel, despite the rushing water, because it had hit the hole sideways. Snowball turned the barrel over several times more and then gave up. She got out of the pool and resumed her pacing. Misty took over the barrel and attempted to get the last fish. She hauled the now full, seven-hundred-pound barrel out of the pool using only her teeth and neck muscles and dumped the water out of the barrel. But the herring did not come out in the rushing water. Eventually, she gave up and resumed her nap.

A clear pattern had emerged through the enrichment events. Snowball was an excellent problem solver and took part in almost everything—seemingly for the sake of the activity, since she didn't always stay for the reward—but returned to pacing instead. Making her life more complex was definitely good for her, but it had no lasting impact on her pacing. It seemed as if she had no choice but to return to pacing time and again.

If her pacing was a compulsion that she *had* to practice, and she wasn't pacing because there was nothing else to do, then it stood to reason that she would only be able to do so many enrich-ment events before she'd *have* to return to pacing. To test this hypothesis, over the next few days I gave Snowball one activity after another, starting first thing in the morning. There was no down time between events. I started the day with activities that she liked and moved onto activities that she loved so that it would be harder to turn away to pace. Whenever she left an activity to go pace, I immediately called her off her pacing path with another activity. Again, a clear pattern emerged. Starting at seven AM, Snowball was only able to participate in four to five events, and then it seemed that she had to return to pacing, usu-ally around noon. She would linger over the first couple of events, then the time spent on each additional activity would decrease as she would quickly eat or finish whatever the task was and return to pacing. Invariably, by the time we got to event number three, it proved more and more difficult to call her off the pacing path. This led to another question. How could one truly know if she was *feeling a compulsion* to pace, or if she was just *choosing* to pace because these activities were boring for a polar bear?

I hoped to answer that question using ice cream. Throughout the summer, it had become apparent that vanilla ice cream was her all-time favorite thing. If I enriched the daylights out of her to the point where she stopped participating in activities and seemed firmly entrenched in her pacing, would she—could she—come off the path for vanilla ice cream?

The next day I called Snowball off her pacing path and offered her and Misty several enrichment activities back-to-back. Snowball responded to the first two, but by the third event, she lingered on the path while turning her head to watch

Misty take part in the scatter feed of berries, nuts, and insects. Finally, she stopped pacing and joined in. When she returned to her pacing path, I called her off for squidsicles. I called and called to her, and, eventually, she reluctantly came over to fish them out of the pool. When she returned to her pacing path, I called her off again for a fifth activity.

This time she kept pacing. She had now reached the ceiling of events that she could participate in. She was pacing on the lip of the pool, and I was being ignored. I dropped a baseball-size wad of vanilla ice cream just past her reach on the pacing pathway, and then another and another. Snowball would have to stop pacing to walk over and lick up the ice cream. I called her name repeatedly, telling her to come for the ice cream, gently encouraging her and obviously bothering her. She paced back and forth faster—mechanically, anxiously—but could not get herself off the pacing path. She looked at the balls of ice cream melting under the hot sun on the cement. Without missing a step, she looked up at me and I saw that she was drooling. It broke my heart. Drooling—it meant that she wanted to have the ice cream, that she was completely conscious and aware of her surroundings while pacing back and forth, but she had a compulsion so strong it could keep her from doing what she would like to do— eat the ice cream. I realized then that enrichment programming had no permanent effect on her pacing and that I had to better understand this demon that was stealing her life.

CHAPTER 5

POLAR BEAR ON PROZAC

Snowball Gets Her Life Back

IT WAS REPEATABLE: no matter how often I attempted to call Snowball off her pacing path for vanilla ice cream after she had maxed out on enrichment activities, she could not break her pace long enough to eat the ice cream. She would watch it melt as she anxiously increased her pacing speed, back and forth, drooling.

We kept the enrichment program in place, and I switched my focus to the pacing itself. To solve the problem, I first had to understand it. To understand it, I first had to describe it, then look for similar phenomena somewhere else. I scheduled four-hour observation sessions at various times throughout the day, three days a week, for three weeks.

Within the first few sessions, I learned that Snowball had four pacing pathways in her cement fortress. She paced on the lip of the north pool wall, on the west rim of the pebble pool, in front of the west viewing windows, and on the lip of the west pool wall, where she spent the vast majority of her time pacing. I guessed that was because it gave her a long, uninterrupted view through the exhibit windows down a main thoroughfare into the zoo. As she paced, she would orient her head in the direction of the windows. Since the tundra and pack ice offer wild polar bears open spaces with long-distance views, it stands to reason that she might be genetically inclined to seek such a view. Or perhaps she preferred that path because the pool was usually full to the brim, and cool water would wash over her feet into the pebble pool beneath, a huge asset when you are pacing on a hot summer's day.

This path had one other very important feature: it was high enough off the ground and far enough back from the twenty-five-foot-high enclosure wall that a bear could smell the west wind as it eddied and dropped informational scents into the bear pit. The enclosure walls were a formidable barrier against the wind and created a huge informational vacuum in the pit. Most animals—particularly bears—use wind-borne information about their surroundings to orient themselves. A bear's sense of smell is the primary sense on which he relies. For humans, it's our sense of sight. If we are burning toast for breakfast while in the bathroom, our sense of smell alerts us to the fact that we may be going to Tim Hortons on the way to work instead, but it is our vision that gives us our final, indisputable verdict—yes, the toast is so burned that it can't even be scraped back into a breakfast food. Seeing is believing. For a bear, smelling is believing, and he will confirm information gathered visually with a smell check.

When Snowball was pacing on the west pool wall—which she was much of her day—she would take exactly six regimented walking steps south, then turn 180 degrees and take six regimented steps north. During the turn, she would suddenly twitch her masseter and temporal chewing muscles while huffing or coughing in a way that sounded like the rushing of expulsed air from her lungs.[1] As she repeated this pattern, her feet fell in exactly the same locations that they had the time before. She could repeat this routine anywhere from a couple of times to hundreds of times before taking a break, depending on how entrenched she was in the behavior.

In the still of daybreak, as the sun cracked open the night, Snowball would stretch, get up, locate Misty, go to the pool, get a drink, wash her face, and then get on her pacing path and begin her day. Pacing defined her day.

On a particularly cold, frustrating morning, I arrived at the zoo late. Snowball had already gotten up and was now deeply entrenched in her pace on the west pool wall. She had seen me as I watched her with my stopwatch, paper, and pencil—coffee in hand—counting the number of rotations and the duration of each bout. I could count until I was blue in the face—which I would be if I continued to stay outside—but I wasn't getting anywhere. *Why* was she doing this? What was she getting out of it? *What was it like?* Bingo: What was it like? That was a good question. In desperation, I moved to the viewing windows inside, because it was warmer there and I didn't want anyone other than Snowball to see me. *What was it like?* The only way to find out was to pace.

Even though I was alone in the polar bear building, I felt self-conscious, silly, and afraid that someone might think I had lost my mind. But I did it anyway, not really expecting much from the experience. I had a few false starts and stops, trying to figure out exactly how to pace. I tried counting my steps to mimic Snowball's pattern, but my mind wandered and I kept losing count. Frustrated, I started to walk up and down the long public viewing hall, ignoring the number of steps. At first, I was completely aware of my surroundings and noticed that Snowball was watching me every time her pace was oriented south and she could see through the window. We were pacing in sync. Soon, I was lost in my thoughts. I figured that if a security guard came by, I would simply explain what I was doing. He wouldn't think I was odd. Who was I kidding? I thought I was odd. Then my thoughts moved out of the present and into problem solving. I remembered my father telling me that my grandfather—who was an arson detective—would pace up and down the hall, chewing on his pipe, mulling over a particularly difficult case.

Snowball moved off her pacing path. That brought me back to my surroundings, and I stopped to watch her. Suddenly I realized a couple of things: that my body had automatically regimented my steps—unconsciously, I had been taking six forward and six back—and I had a small sense of euphoria. I wasn't too surprised that my body had chosen to regiment my otherwise random steps; it seemed like a resourceful strategy for a body. But feeling a sense of euphoria was a big surprise, especially since I had just been feeling grievously annoyed by my lack of progress. I made notes. A change in feeling meant a change in my biochemistry, and a change in my biochemistry meant something neurological.

Snowball reminded me of a close friend who had had a repetitive hand-washing behavior. His symptoms showed up when he began to take doctor-prescribed corticosteroids. During this period, he suffered a great deal of anguish—his greatest fear was that people would think he had lost his mind. Logically, he knew that his hands were clean, but his brain kept repeating the same message: that they were dirty and needed washing. So he would wash them again and again, trying desperately to get the "clean hands" message to register in his brain. He had no control over his anxious need to repeatedly wash his hands. His obsessive-compulsive behavior faded away when he stopped taking the corticosteroids.

My grandfather *chose* to pace when he wanted to concentrate on a case. He could start and stop at will. He gave it no real thought, and it played no major role in his life. My friend had little or no control over his repetitive behavior; he became anxious if he couldn't wash his hands but was troubled because he did not want to keep washing them. He wanted the internal message (the obsession) and the external behavior (the compulsion) to stop.

Clearly, pacing had many possible causes, just as a runny nose can be caused by an allergy, a cold day, a cold or the flu, or a pea stuck up a child's nostril. Snowball's behavior seemed more like my friend's behavior; after she at first deflected her need to pace with other activities, she eventually *had* to get back to it.

Judith Rapoport, chief of the Child Psychiatry Branch at the National Institute of Mental Health in the United States, reported that the unwilling and seemingly endless repetition of behaviors that we are genetically programmed to perform in appropriate circumstances, such as grooming (hand washing) or hoarding (storing food items and nesting materials), indicates that there is a biological malfunction of the basal ganglia, the place of origin in the brain for these inherent behaviors.[2] People who suffer from these repetitive behaviors have obsessive-compulsive disorder (OCD). It is estimated that 20 percent of human sufferers of OCD also have facial tics[3] similar to Snowball's grimace.

I took my suspicions about Snowball's behavior to Cam Teskey, a remarkable neuroscientist at the University of Calgary who is well known for his work in neural plasticity—and who didn't throw me out of his office for being a nut. An out-of-the-box thinker, Teskey felt the idea had merit and suggested that we test the hypothesis. He developed a study procedure, protocols, and data analysis.

In the interim, zoo staff made enclosure renovations for Snowball and Misty to further complicate their environment and to accommodate the enrichment program.[4] Like other species of bears, polar bears dig day beds into snow or sandy soil or rake together seaweed and vegetation to create a nest for naps and whole sleeps. They sleep, on average, seven hours and forty-five minutes per day—similar to what a human needs.[5] Snowball had never felt anything other than cement, ice, and snow under her feet. Misty had spent a year in the wild with her mother, but I wondered what recollection, if any, she had of digging day beds in the tundra.

To create a more natural environment, we were going to fill the pebble pool to the brim with truckloads of woodchips, which we hoped the bears would use as a day bed. One morning, for the first time since the building was opened, we turned off the cascading waterfall. The white noise of the rushing water had drowned out natural sounds like birdsong and other animal calls. We removed most of the pebbles and refilled the pool with woodchips. Snowball and Misty had been locked in the back, listening to the noise of trucks and front-end loaders. Finally, by late afternoon, we gave them access to their refurbished exhibit. A small group of well-wishers gathered to watch as both bears came straight out.

Snowball approached the woodchip bed first. Misty stayed behind Snowball, who slowly, carefully moved forward to the edge of the pool, stretched her neck, and took several long reconnaissance breaths over the woodchips. Then she stuck her nose right into the bed. She lifted her right paw and placed it on the chips, pressed slightly, and then quickly pulled it back. She was smiling and—like most other bears I have observed who are suddenly faced with a smorgasbord of smells to decipher—she was drooling, and her nose was running as her olfactory and salivary glands worked overtime.

Snowball pretend-walked onto the woodchips with her front paws—right, then left—keeping her rear paws firmly planted on the cement floor. She brought her right paw up, turned it over, sniffed it, and visually checked the pad. It was a poignant moment. I couldn't stop the tears from trilling down my face. Then she checked the pad on the left paw. Drying vagrant tears with my jacket sleeve, I vowed that her life would never be so invariable and banal again. Snowball tobogganed on her belly onto the woodchips, keeping her rear feet on the cement—presumably in case she had to make a quick retreat from offensive woodchips. We all collapsed with laughter. Then Snowball rolled onto her back, all four feet in the air, and proceeded to roll over and over, bathing in woodchips and woodchip scent.

Misty stood by motionless, carefully observing Snowball. Suddenly she rushed across the woodchip bed with exaggerated steps, as if she were walking on lit briquettes. She leapt safely onto the cement lip of the other side and did not return to the pit for the rest of the day. Misty acclimated herself to the bed overnight, rolling over and over in it. The following morning, I greeted one white polar bear (Snowball had washed in the pool) and what could have passed for one brown bear if I hadn't known better.

The bears dug day beds in the woodchip bed and searched for scattered foods. The natural substrate attracted squirrels, who could be chased or just watched depending on what mood a bear was in. As expected, the improvements to the enclosure did not reduce or eradicate Snowball's pacing behavior, and we proceeded with our research.

Repetitive behaviors—also called stereotypies—are exhibited not just by humans and bears but also by a myriad of other species, such as spinning cats, tail-chasing dogs, brachiating monkeys, cribbing horses, and bar-gnawing pigs. Each individual repeats a unique behavioral pattern that can be expressed more or less often and can be more or less entrenched into its daily routine. Stereotypies can be caused by drugs, brain damage or malfunction, or impoverished environments; the last is likely most often the case for zoo animals.[6]

There is usually an immediate cause-and-effect relationship between a stereotypy and a bear's issue. Once you understand the issue, the stereotypy can be quickly remedied. For example, a bear may pace in response to being locked out of her bedrooms during the day to keep her on exhibit for public viewing, a practice that was and still is common in some zoos. Bears view all of their enclosure as theirs, and being denied access to part of their territory causes them distress. In response, a bear will pace quite persistently—for days or weeks if she has to—until the access door is opened. Then the pacing stops. The bear usually runs in to check the area, then comes back out and resumes normal behavior, leaving the keeper to wonder what all the fuss was about. Imagine if someone locked you out of your bedroom during the day. We call it home invasion and consider it criminal. Bears are every bit as invested in their land as we are in ours.

Snowball's initial stressor—aggressive males—was removed years ago. She was left with an unchanging, barren environment, and over time her pacing became divorced from her current environment[7] and immune to positive change. It was its own entity. Similarly, my hand-washing friend could have moved to a million-dollar condo in Hawaii, but he would still have been forced to wash his hands. The link between Snowball's problem and my friend's OCD was likely their brain serotonergic system.[8] Serotonin is a neurotransmitter, an information-carrying chemical that crosses over the space (or synapse) between the nerve cell (or neuron) that releases the chemical and another nerve cell that receives it on a specialized receptor site. If something messes with this process, like brain damage or a drug, information transfer is impaired. The affected person wants to stop washing his hands, but his brain does not pick up the "clean hands" message.

The brain serotonergic system is implicated because human OCD patients and animals with chronic stereotypies are responsive to a family of drugs called selective serotonin reuptake inhibitors, or SSRIs.[9] In a compromised process, serotonin is released by the neuron and then received by a receptor site on that same neuron. In other words, the bus went around the block and then came back—it didn't go anywhere. The SSRI will keep the first cell from binding to the serotonin that it released for transfer to the second cell, meaning that the bus leaves the station and arrives at its destination. We chose to work with the SSRI fluoxetine—Prozac—because it is a highly selective compound that affects only the serotonergic system and has fewer side effects than clomipramine, the other leading drug prescribed for OCD at the time. Prozac is most commonly thought of as an antidepressant, but mood does not play a role in OCD—you do not have to suffer from depression to have OCD, and antidepressants other than SSRIs are not effective in treating OCD.[10]

Teskey developed a standard three-phase ("ABA") study procedure to test whether Prozac, in concert with the environmental enrichment program and the redesign of the enclosure to incorporate natural features, had an effect on Snowball's pacing and other abnormal behaviors. No one in the study group, which included a neuroscientist, a veterinarian, a zoo manager, and a zookeeper, believed it was ethical to leave an animal in a lifeless environment, load her up on drugs, and say, "Here—cope!" In the first phase, A, we would describe Snowball's behaviors before medical therapy. During the second phase, B, we would describe Snowball's behaviors with fluoxetine. In the last phase, A, we would describe Snowball's behaviors without fluoxetine. This evaluation process would help us assess if Prozac could benefit Snowball.

The entire study, including all three phases, lasted three hundred days, beginning in July 1994 and ending in May 1995. In the first phase, which lasted thirty-two days, we videotaped Snowball's behavior every third day for nine hours, from seven AM to four PM. A master's student, Pamela Valentine, tallied the amount of time Snowball spent in stereotypic mobility (pacing or other stereotypy), in non-stereotypic mobility (gross movement but not pacing or other stereotypy), in immobility while awake (standing, sitting, or lying still with head up), asleep (recumbent with head down), and off camera. The camera angle included approximately 85 percent of the outdoor enclosure.

We found out that Snowball paced 68.6 percent of her day. Typically, she initiated a pacing bout about twenty-two times a day, and each bout lasted an average of almost seventeen minutes. In those seventeen minutes, she could pace about seventy-eight cycles (back and forth), and each cycle took thirteen seconds to complete.[11] Snowball's facial tic and snorting were consistently displayed at every turn. She favored the west pool wall but switched paths seemingly to follow the shade.

What had not been apparent in my initial observations but was revealed on the videotapes was that Snowball had a second repetitive pattern. She would repeat an entire behavioral planning sequence of pace-swim-pace. This sequence could have been initiated, and been beneficial to her, since she could easily overheat. In his book *Polar Bears*, Ian Stirling states that a wild bear travelling up to two and a half miles per hour in temperatures of five to minus thirteen degrees Fahrenheit can maintain a normal body temperature of ninety-nine degrees Fahrenheit.[12] Snowball typically paced at 2.2 miles per hour in weather warmer than five degrees Fahrenheit. She would periodically need to cool off in a hurry, and a quick dip in the pool would help her do that.

The treatment phase, B, lasted 106 days. First thing in the morning, we would stuff Prozac capsules into the gill slits of four or five herring and hand-feed the fish to Snowball to be certain that she got the pills. We administered the drug on an allometric scale: slowly increasing the dose until the pacing completely stopped. When her blood serum levels of fluoxetine and its likely active metabolite, norfluoxetine, reached those typically therapeutic for humans, Snowball's stereotypic patterns—pacing and the pace-swim-pace routine—ceased, and she replaced them with typical polar bear behaviors.[13] Her facial tic and snorting, which had been expressed only when she was pacing, disappeared also.

Over the years, Snowball had developed a consistent annual pattern of fur loss in the winter months, September to May, and fur regrowth in the summer months, June, July, and August. Every fall she would lose most of her guard hairs—the long, usually coarse, protective hairs over her short, soft undercoat. Then she would lose parts of her undercoat on both flanks and sometimes over her shoulders. We were surprised and delighted to discover that while Snowball was on Prozac both her undercoat and her guard hairs grew back, and she was fully furred in the fall of 1994 through the winter of 1995–96.

Instead of pacing for 68.6 percent of her waking hours, she now took part in enrichment throughout the day, swam in the pool, and watched zoo visitors. Snowball seemed to have more time on her paws. She was relaxed and lingered over enrichment activities instead of racing to finish the task and then running off to pace. There was a definite downside for Misty, however, as Snowball often stayed to eat the rewards.

The day after her pacing completely ceased, I gave the bears several puzzle feeders, which they had to manipulate so that the raisins, peanuts, and mealworms inside would drop out. Misty worked on one and Snowball worked on the other. Misty had depleted hers of every last morsel in about an hour. She expectantly sauntered over and began to maneuver the feeder that Snowball had left—but it was empty! She peered over at Snowball, who was busy rolling in the woodchips.

A mentally and physically healthy bear is a bear that is self-possessed and constantly evaluates what the environment holds for her, whether that's finding the shadiest and coolest place to have a nap or retrieving any and all of the watermelons in the pool.

The first time I tossed watermelons into the pool after Snowball had stopped pacing, a whole new scenario unfolded. As usual, Snowball immediately jumped into the pool to retrieve both watermelons, and Misty waited on deck for Snowball's return. With one watermelon under each arm, Snowball slowly paddled back toward the pool's edge. Observing Misty on deck waiting for her, she rerouted her landing away from Misty. The message was clear: Snowball was avoiding Misty and keeping the watermelons for herself. Misty stood still and watched, then retreated to the shade to continue her nap. Watermelons were a coveted item that both bears liked. Now, suddenly, there were not enough for both of them.

A few days later, I dropped three watermelons into the pool. Snowball jumped in immediately, buoyed one under each arm, and rerouted her return back to the deck away from where Misty was standing. As was typical, Misty had showed up at the pool's edge. She watched Snowball break open one of her melons and begin to devour it. The third melon was floating around in the middle of the pool. As if trying to make a decision, Misty looked alternately at the yet-unclaimed melon and at Snowball, who completely ignored her. Eventually, Misty dove into the pool for the last watermelon. Suddenly things had changed. In a non-overt but assertive manner, Snowball had become more competitive, more able to reap the natural benefits of her behavior. Misty would no longer be able to grab Snowball's leftover rewards.

In the final, nontreatment phase, A, we stopped giving Snowball Prozac so we could accurately assess the drug's effect. This phase lasted for 138 observation days. In the first four months after treatment, from November 1994 to March 1995, Snowball was almost pacing-free. Very quickly, though, it became apparent to me that the behavior was likely going to return in some form.

Exactly eight days after we had ceased treatment, I looked at Snowball as I was passing by doing something else. She was walking from the building, past the pool, down to the west viewing windows. Amid her normal relaxed, lumbering steps, there suddenly appeared—in a split second—one single, stiff, mechanized, pacing goose-step. Then she returned to normal relaxed, lumbering steps. I stood there not quite believing what I had just seen. Although I questioned my gut interpretation of this event and even whether I had actually seen it, I recorded the incident.

Since Snowball's successful treatment, she had been able to spend more time bonding with me. She would often come up to watch me when I was working in the back of the building, and I would reward her with treats. If she noticed me walk into the public viewing area, she would come up to the window to look at me. On her way over, she would raise her head up at me briefly and sniff a greeting, and I would do the same. A few weeks after I noticed the single goose-step, Snowball came up to the window to greet me. Instead of her usual head bob, out came her facial tic and huffing noise, and then she immediately resumed her normal appearance. There it was again, another split-second, fragmented intrusion of her past behavior. I made note of it and began to trust these observations, which unfortunately increased in frequency. Like so many pieces in a puzzle, the small, momentary intrusions eventually coalesced into the old pacing pattern. In the meantime, a human drama was unfolding, too.

In January 1995, while we were in the final phase of the study, a reporter for the *Calgary Herald* caught wind of our work with Snowball and wrote a front-page article about Snowball on Prozac. Other outlets picked up the story, and sexy, newspaper-selling headlines about "polar bears on Prozac" appeared around the globe. Reporters assumed that Snowball was being treated for depression. Everyone had an opinion. Words like "neurotic," "depressed," "psychotic," and "insane"—words that most of us do not truly know the meaning of—were accusingly spat out.

Graham Harrop, cartoonist responsible for the political comic strip *BackBench*, published several cartoons dedicated to polar bears and penguins on Prozac. I was depicted as a little male zookeeper in a traditional zookeeper suit plus hat, with a Hitler-style mustache and a butterfly net, who was attempting to con a captive polar bear and his penguin friends into taking their daily Prozac because it was better than electroshock therapy—which is what the animals would get if they didn't behave. Harrop borrowed the festive tone from *One Flew Over the Cuckoo's Nest*.

The subject popped up everywhere. In an article titled "Women in '95," published in the January 1996 issue of *Chatelaine* magazine, a report on Snowball, the female polar bear on Prozac, appeared along with reports on Silken Laumann, who unfortunately lost her gold medal from the Pan American Games for using a decongestant; the fact that more women than men were dying from smoking-related deaths and breast cancer. I was told that the *Late Show* had called and wanted to know if we were interested in talking about the issue on the show. Although I was and still am a huge fan of David Letterman, there was no way that I could have discussed this issue with a comedian and expected something meaningful to come out of it. We respectfully declined.

Zoo staff—some less than happy with me—had to field questions from the public about the use of Prozac. I noticed, though, that zoo visitors were very supportive of our efforts to help Snowball, once they had the facts.

I was watching Snowball and Misty hunting around for their scattered treats when a woman approached me and asked which bear was Snowball. I pointed her out. The woman came closer and very quietly told me that she had suffered from obsessive-compulsive disorder for years but was now taking an ssri and had found relief. She had suffered in silence because of the stigma attached to mental illness, and she was afraid that people, including her relatives, would think that she was neurotic, depressed, psychotic, and insane. In tears, she told me that when she found out that Snowball had been diagnosed with obsessive-compulsive disorder–like symptoms and had responded positively to the same treatment that she was receiving, she knew it meant that she wasn't crazy. This was a legitimate disease with a legitimate treatment. This woman was the first of about a dozen zoo visitors who told me similar, heartrending stories.

I was honored and deeply humbled that each person would entrust me with such personal information, which in the wrong hands could cause them unimaginable embarrassment and grief. I was also deeply saddened, because if they had to share this information with a stranger, it meant that there was probably no one safe to tell within their own sphere. It was heartening that our work to help Snowball was also helping people affected by obsessive-compulsive disorder.

By April, Snowball was back to pacing every day, and by May, she was spending as much time pacing as she had before the treatment, and the repetitive patterns had been recovered exactly as they were before treatment. Snowball went back to being too busy to spend much time with me. She left treats behind, Misty ate them, and there was again a ceiling on the number of enrichment activities Snowball could take part in before she had to pace. We had all agreed that if the treatment plus the enrichment programming and enclosure redesign gave Snowball a better quality of life, we would continue the regime after the study. Before we could consider this option, however, our veterinarians had to deal with another issue.

In the post-treatment phase, Snowball had periodically shown some lameness in her left rear leg and hip. She was now twenty-seven years old, and we thought she might have developed arthritis. We treated her with anti-inflammatory drugs, which did help her initially, but the condition worsened over time. Snowball had developed severe arthritis of the hip joints, and, because of her advanced years and her condition, we decided that it would be best to euthanize her.

The night before, I had to betray my friend and entice her to come inside to spend the night in a bedroom in which I had left treats and a deep bed of fresh straw. Snowball trustingly came inside and lay down in the warm straw. I sat next to her for a while and lingered by talking to her and doing pretend odd jobs.

I didn't want to alarm her unnecessarily. Eventually, I ran out of excuses and left. It was late, and the sun had set, and as I walked around the building past the west viewing windows I could just make out Misty lying down outside by the double door that led to Snowball's bedroom. Misty could not see Snowball, but I assumed that she could smell her. Why was she lying there? Snowball and Misty were both completely familiar with this routine, which usually led to a veterinary checkup the next morning. Misty had not lain by the door on the other side of Snowball's bedroom before.

I arrived at work very early the next morning to spend as much time as possible with Snowball before the veterinary staff arrived at eight. As I approached the building, I could just make out Misty's form sleeping by Snowball's double door. She had been there all night.

CHAPTER 6

CONVERSATIONS WITH A POLAR BEAR

Misty Asks for Stuff

A FEW DAYS after Snowball died, I had the feeling I was being stared at and turned to see Misty standing in the doorway. She had done this when Snowball was still alive, preferring to let Snowball do all of the interacting with humans. Although I had known Misty for years, now that Snowball had died I wanted to establish a closer bond with her. I got out the peanuts that I normally carried in my pocket, crouched down by the gate, and softly called her name. But Misty walked away. OK then—next time. I repeated this overture for several days, and I always left a few peanuts as my calling card, which she sometimes retrieved. Finally, Misty, like Snowball before her, came up to me while I sat there. She offered no smiles, no goofy playful behavior—she just stared, testing me. I moved slowly and quietly, frequently averted my eyes so that I wasn't staring right at her, and often feigned interest in minuscule bits of junk on the floor—I had learned this from the grizzlies—while I sat crouched. And I always offered treats.

At first, Misty would plant her back legs firmly in the doorway and stretch her body cautiously forward until her belly rested on the ground to reach the peanuts. With her back legs stationary and her body completely elongated, she had quite a reach—just under ten feet. Misty often did this when she was confronted with new things. I dubbed it the "extend-a-bear" behavior. Although Misty wasn't the only bear who extended her body this way, she was definitely a master at it; she could snap back and take off within a millisecond if she had to. Eventually she moved her whole body closer to the gate where I sat and ate the peanuts that I threw on the floor. She ignored my offers to hand-feed her until two weeks into the process. Then one day, a determined and speedy Misty marched right up to the gate, took the peanut from my hand, and quickly backed out of the building, dropping the peanut as she turned, and left huffing. It reminded me of her reconnaissance run across the woodchip bed. I wondered if she was huffing because she was mad at me or because she was stressed and needed to huff off her anxiety. There was no reason to be angry with me—except for the unforgivable fact that I was human. She didn't have to take a peanut from my hand, since I had tossed plenty on the floor as an alternative source to relieve some of our introduction stress. She must have perceived a benefit in connecting with me that was greater than the acquisition of peanuts. I suspect that, in part, she needed to socialize, and now, sadly, I was the only game in town. Female polar bears spend a great deal of their life with family members. I'd have to do, even though I was of another species.

Being chronically opportunistic, bears will get what they need from whatever source is available. In his book *The World of the Polar Bear*, Norbert Rosing has published a now classic series of photographs of a young wild male polar bear playing with an Inuit sled dog tied up outside. The bear visited the dog for ten consecutive days to play-fight.[1] This scenario could have begun or ended tragically for the dog, but clearly the polar bear perceived a benefit in rolling, wrestling, and play-fighting.

While Snowball was alive, we had noticed that Misty—like wild polar bears in the southern regions of their range—was seasonally active. In the summer she was inactive, spending much of her time resting on the cool cement floor in the building bedrooms. She would come out to participate in enrichment events, but overall she became picky about foods, eating only favorites, such as watermelons, ice treats, and berries, if she ate at all. In the fall and winter, Misty's activity levels and her appetite dramatically increased, and she paced. Unlike Snowball, who paced steadily every day, Misty could go for days without pacing. Then suddenly, without any noticeable precursors, she would pace for a few consecutive days at normal speed—2.2 miles per hour— just like Snowball.

On rare occasions, possibly twice a season, Misty would launch into a frantic pacing bout, speed-walking at three to four miles per hour, without stopping to eat or sleep, for up to three days in a row. She broke from the pace only to swim across the pool, presumably to cool off, and then she would hop back onto the pacing path as though it were a treadmill. When we threw any of her favorite foods, such as a whole chicken, onto the path to entice her to stop pacing and eat, she would kick them aside or crush them into a pulp under her racing feet. These extreme episodes seemed steeped in anxiety and, oddly enough, fear. We later learned that Misty was prone to seizures.

After Snowball's death, Misty took to pacing all of the time, including during the summer months. Our holistic approach to helping Snowball and Misty—now just Misty—was to improve the external environment (the enclosure) as well as the internal one (the bears' health). We proceeded with plans to continue refurbishing the old exhibit. Our objective was to put as many natural elements into the cement pit as possible. We planned to fill the entire exhibit with woodchips, place giant boulders in the pool to create relief topography, bring in additional tree trunks for climbing, and build Misty a den in the outside enclosure for shade and protection from the elements.

In early June 1996, Jim Price (now head foreman of animal care) and I went shopping at the sewer department of the City of Calgary. We were looking for two interlocking cement culverts about four feet in diameter and length with a six-inch lip on one end and a six-inch sleeve on the other. Gently used would be fine. The maintenance yard boss had heard that Snowball had died and wanted to help make life better for Misty. He found exactly what we needed—no charge—and they delivered. This was most often the case when I attempted to procure free stuff for a bear: people wanted to help. Rarely have I been turned away empty-handed. Price organized five loads of woodchips, six tree trunks, a dump truck, a crane, a backhoe, operators, and staff. We were ready.

On the morning of the complete enclosure makeover, I locked Misty in the back with her bedrooms full of straw, enrichment, and treats. We threw the utility doors open and got to work. The crane operator moved most of the boulders off the exhibit floor and skillfully piled them into pyramids that leaned against several corners of the deep pool to vary the depth of the water, create steps, and provide hiding places for live fish. When the air was clear of incoming boulders, our welder replaced the drain covers with finer-mesh grates in our time-tested, bearproof method: he welded them shut. The backhoe operator was busy for hours bringing in load after load to make the entire front end of the pit three feet deep in woodchips. Then he dug a ten-foot-long and two-foot-deep channel.

Everyone scattered when the crane operator returned with a cement culvert swinging from the crane arm. He placed the culvert in one end of the channel. Then he maneuvered the sleeve end of the second culvert over the lip end of the first as the backhoe operator lifted it slightly. Boom—the two culverts were joined, and both operators gently placed their loads in the woodchip bed. The crane operator brought in five more boulders and placed them on the sides and back of the now ten-foot-long culvert to stabilize it. Then he placed several more boulders on top of the structure, creating a little hill, and placed one boulder on each side of the front of the den, effectively extending it another two feet. The backhoe operator completed the project by dumping buckets of woodchips on top of the den, filling in all of the cavities and partly insulating it. The crane operator dropped several more conifers into the exhibit, strategically locating them so that they served as climbing structures or natural bridges. We were finished.

We accounted for all of our tools, counted heads, closed the giant doors, and locked up the fortress. It was after five PM and time for Misty to see what all the commotion was about. She stood in the doorway for several minutes, taking in the new scents of fresh woodchips, trees, incoming water blasting soil off the boulders as it filled the pool, machinery, and human sweat. Cautiously, Misty walked out behind the pool, raised her nose high, and visibly breathed in. She was smiling. She checked out the boulders in the pool. She walked down the north path, stopping briefly here and there to sniff woodchips and tree trunks. Then she saw the den, picked up speed, walked around to the entrance, and sniffed the ground in front of it. Suddenly, Misty did her extend-a-bear routine, stretching her torso into the darkness of the den, keeping her back feet planted at the entrance with her rear end sticking out like a cork in a bottle. She backed out quickly and looked around as if expecting something else to happen, perhaps a door to close behind her. Then she walked into the den, turned around, and came out headfirst. We cheered in relief from our vantage point inside the building; a den isn't much good if a bear can't turn around in it.

Misty walked around the sides, smelling woodchips and boulders. She rose up on her hind legs and slammed her upper torso onto the cement culvert with her front paws, in a typical polar bear ice-breaking maneuver. It held. I was relieved. She went back inside and dug down to the culvert wall, woodchips flying out of the entrance past her rear end. Her face was covered with dirt when she came back out. She was still smiling as she walked over to a conifer trunk. Using her teeth, she ripped off a piece of bark, chewed it briefly, and spat it out. Misty roamed around the exhibit smelling, testing, digging, and smiling until the sun set.

The next morning I came to work early, anxious to see where Misty had spent the night. I couldn't find her—never a good thing—so I called her. Immediately she popped out of the den entrance, covered in dirt and looking like a brown bear. She met me at the window. I crouched down, and we spent time together. She looked at me without taking her eyes off of mine. Her face, though dirty, was relaxed. I thought we were sharing a moment, but in retrospect, I believe she might have come to an understanding that turned the tables on both of us: that I could get her stuff—stuff that she could use.

In my old way of thinking about bear husbandry, I kind of thought that I was in charge and that I would entice Misty to nest build by offering her several types of bedding materials. My objective was to get her to nest build herself. She was an adult who had been taught as a cub, for at least a year that we knew of, by a wild mother. I was certain that she had learned something then about fending for herself. In the southwest corner of the exhibit, I left her bales of straw and hay and a giant gnarl of wood wool—all fine nesting materials, or so I thought.

Immediately, Misty raked flakes of straw into the den and fluffed and fussed. I could hear her huffing periodically—talking to herself. She went over to a tree trunk and ripped off a stiff conifer branch, which she also brought into the den. Then she came back out and brought a mouthful of hay over to the window and ate part of it in front of me. Since wild polar bears will eat vegetation in the summer, I first assumed that she was having a social eat with me. But it is possible that Misty was showing me that hay was for eating, not for nest building.

The wood wool ended up in the pool. When it was wet, it behaved an awful lot like a clump of seaweed, and Misty played with it endlessly by diving off a boulder and coming up wearing it draped over her head and other body parts. Initially, when Misty spotted me coming, she would dive into the pool and display her antics with the wood wool. Unlike seaweed, wood wool comes apart easily with handling, and I'd have to go fishing for small gobs in the pool and filtration system. I brought her a new bunch, and we'd start over again.

I wondered about the conifer branch. It didn't seem soft enough to work as bedding, so I brought Misty several seven-foot, springy willow branches from the edge of the Bow River. She immediately took them, ate the crisp leaves, broke down the branches, and incorporated them into her nest building.

Misty set up her own daily routine, which I now worked around. Except for the rare appearance of the extreme, three-day marathons, daily pacing seemed to be a thing of the past. On a typical day, Misty would get up, have a drink, wash her face, and then search for leftover foods from the day before. By this time I would have arrived, and I would ask her to come to the back for treats and bonding. I'd close her in long enough for me to clean the outside enclosure and put down enrichment and breakfast. When she came out, she would eat her favorite foods first and then go to refresh her nest. Nest fluffing could take up to an hour of adjusting and rearranging. After this, she took a midday nap, which usually lasted several hours. In the afternoon and evening, she would alternate her time between investigating fresh enrichment, standing on the west pool wall breathing in airborne information on the west winds, swimming, playing, and napping some more.

Once every seven to ten days, Misty cleaned out the entire den. Sweeping aggressively with her paws, she sent old straw, woodchips, and branch bits flying out of the den, forming a pile of junk in front of the entrance for me to clean up the next morning. Misty then raked flakes from the fresh bale of straw I had given her into the den and brought over springy new willow branches, which she broke into usable pieces. The entire nest rejuvenation process took most of the day.

Misty seemed extremely fastidious about nest cleanliness, which included pausing at the entrance to knock off bits of dirt from her foot pads before entering. I had hesitated to go into her den because it was her private domain, where she seemed to thrive. The fact that she could come and go as she pleased there and no one could ever close her in gave her, I believe, enormous relief and comfort. I really wasn't certain that my scent and I were welcome in there, but I needed a quick reassurance that Misty was keeping it as clean as she seemed to be. So I pulled an extend-a-bear maneuver and stuck my upper torso inside for a quick inspection with just my rear end sticking out—yup— like a cork in a bottle. The nest was a work of art. It was built in layers. The bottom was composed of a layer of soil, crushed woodchips, and straw bits no longer than an inch or two. The middle was a layer of springy willow branches, and the top layer was made of fluffy, fresh straw, which is what she turned over every day. Cached in the back were a bone and a couple of apples, still in pretty good shape. There were no feces or wet, urine-soaked straw: everything was orderly and clean. If it hadn't been for the fact that this was someone else's den, I would have gladly taken a nap.

It had been a busy time. The enclosure renovation had put me behind on other projects for other animals. I was beetling past the viewing windows, going someplace else, when Misty came running up. Her hurried manner and determined stare demanded my attention. I stopped and gave it to her. Keeping her eyes locked with mine, she backed up to the den entrance, raked some dirty straw, picked it up in her mouth, brought it over, and then dropped it in front of me. Oh great, that was just what I needed: a straw-eating, impacted polar bear. Misty scooped up bits of grungy straw from the little pile with her claws. She tried to hold it up, but it kept falling off. Embarrassingly, testifying to just how slow on the uptake I can be, I was completely perplexed. I was also busy, so I left to do whatever it was that was so important.

Misty had made an impression: I was now concerned. An hour later, I made another pass by the enclosure to check up on her. Again, she hurried over to the window, locked me in with her stare, backed up to the den entrance while still staring at me, raked up a small pile of old straw, picked it up in her mouth, and brought it over to the window. This time she lifted her right paw off the ground and dropped the straw on top of it—some fell off, some stayed. Then it hit me: I had forgotten to give her a new bale of straw. Is that what she was doing—asking for straw? If she was, then this behavior would stop after the straw arrived, and it was important for me to be immediately responsive so that Misty would see a cause and effect.

In a quick change of plan, I got a fresh bale of straw for Misty. To speed things up, I dropped the bale in parts from the upper deck. Misty immediately began raking straw toward the den entrance. I came down from the upper deck to watch her through the viewing windows. Misty briefly stopped what she was doing and turned to look at me. Her face was relaxed, and she was smiling. I smiled back. Then she proceeded to ignore me and go about her cleaning business. So I proceeded to go about mine.

The only way to test whether we had communicated as I thought we had was to see if the experience was repeatable. I purposely let more than seven days go by. Sure enough, Misty again came to the window with a mouthful of dirty straw. This time, I was less stupid about it and responded immediately with a clean bale, which I chucked in from the upper deck. From that time on, I never gave Misty straw unless she requested it. When she did make a request, I responded immediately. Interestingly, Misty refined her request behavior. She had learned that it was enough to simply show up at the window with straw in her mouth. One day I noticed that she had stored a small pile of straw by the window, and she simply ran to it and picked it up when I was racing by. It's likely that I had missed her request earlier that day, and she just dropped it where she was, handy for later use.

One morning, I had just come back downstairs from dropping off straw on the upper deck, when Misty turned up at the window with an old willow stick in her mouth. OK then— gimme a minute! I had to borrow the truck to go cut willow branches for her by the river.

I wasn't always racing by. It was just that Misty's requests for straw and browse usually came in the morning (so that she could spend the day cleaning her den), when I had other bears and animals to clean, feed, and enrich. In the late afternoon, before I went home, we'd sometimes spend up to half an hour just sitting together, she on her side of the window and I on mine. Sometimes she'd look at me, sometimes not. It didn't seem to matter—it was just time spent.

The summer passed. As was usual in Calgary, fall was undetectable, as the temperatures dropped quickly to winter norms. The size of the den had been on my mind. I wondered if it was slightly too big and would allow cold air to circulate around Misty, preventing an envelope of body-generated warm air to hug her. On a warmer day, our welder built a fence structure two feet from the back of the den. It had a trap door so that I could get my arm in to stuff the back full of straw for insulation. It worked extremely well. Misty continued to use her outdoor den at night, during storms, or in extremely cold weather (below minus twenty-two degrees Fahrenheit).

As had been her pattern, Misty now came to life in the winter. I had to stay one step ahead of her need for enrichment and variation. The maintenance crew looked the other way when I allowed the top of the pebble pool to freeze over. Misty spent hours pounding holes in the ice with her front paws, in the typical polar bear ice-breaking maneuver. Then she got creative and rammed barrels, PVC puzzle feeders, and small logs into the ice. Before I left each night, I topped up the pebble pool with water. Every morning it was frozen over, and every afternoon Misty turned it into Swiss cheese.

Late one afternoon, I was racing past the viewing windows when something flying through the air caught my peripheral vision. I turned in time to see a frozen feeder rabbit make a crash landing in a snow bank. *What the—?* Misty stood innocently by the pebble pool, watching me watch her. I pretended to leave, then sneaked back and hid behind a poster display, hoping Misty wouldn't notice that the tripod had five legs, two of which wore work pants.

Misty reared back on her hind legs and crashed her weight-powered front paws into the pebble pool ice, making a rather neat little hole about eighteen inches in diameter. Then she retrieved her feeder rabbit, which, because of its frozen status, was shaped pretty much like a curling rock, with all the limbs and little head tucked in. She plunked the bunny into the water hole, positioned it a little with her paw, and left. Then Misty took what can only be described as a leisurely stroll around the perimeter of the enclosure, always looking away from the pebble pool, first on the south path, then up the west path. As she came around the north side of her enclosure, she turned her head to look at the pool and—freeze-frame—stood stock-still for a second, eyes fixed on the hole in the ice. Slowly, she lowered her head and moved forward, silently stalking. When she was fifteen feet of the pool, she burst into action, bolted forward at blinding speed, leapt onto the hole, and with her paw, slap-shot the imaginary seal right out of its hole, sending the curling-rock bunny flying eighty feet through the air, crashing into the snow, and sliding another thirty feet. I was astounded. Misty raced after it and pretend-chewed its wee head. Having successfully "killed" it, she brought it back to the hole and started the game over.

I made a mental note to always bring Misty frozen feeder rabbits when it was cold enough for the pool to freeze over. But it would be difficult to keep that commitment. Although our commissary keepers had stored up several hundred frozen feeder rabbits, we ran out halfway through the winter. Contrary to popular belief, rabbits are not easy to breed. They require a substantial amount of daylight for their reproductive works to work, and in the dead of winter Calgary has only around seven to eight hours of daylight. Farm rabbits were more inclined to den up than breed this time of year. Undaunted, I dug a whole, frozen, feathered chicken out of the freezer for Misty and chucked it into the enclosure.

The next day, as I was passing by the windows, Misty came running over and stared at me. She seemed anxious and serious. Her mouth was a tiny slit, and her eyes were determined. I stopped and gave her my complete attention. Her eyes locked to mine, then she backed up a few yards and picked up the frozen chicken in her mouth. Then she backed up to the pebble pool, eyes still on mine, and dropped it into an open water hole. She bounced the chicken up and down a few times; the feathers, limbs, and neck loosened and thawed, and the chicken began to float. Misty came up to the window and stared at me. Clearly, Misty was demonstrating something, but I had no idea what it was. I didn't move. Was I supposed to go get something? What?

Frustrated, she performed a mini ice-breaking maneuver while staring at me. She stomped on the ground with both front paws in a tiny but effective front-paw jump-and-stomp. This is a standard bear sign of annoyance or frustration—for Misty, usually involving me.

Misty then took a demonstration stroll around the enclosure, often checking to make certain I was still watching her. I was. Halfway along the north side of the enclosure, Misty froze, then lowered her head, leapt forward onto the pool ice, and slapped that chicken out of the hole—well, only sort of. The thawing chicken flopped onto the ground less than three feet away, feathers, wings, and legs sprawled like wet mop strings on a deck. Even I could feel the disappointment. Misty raised her head and stared at me. I got it—chickens don't work! You can't really get the same oomph behind a soggy chicken that you can with a frozen solid, curling-rock rabbit. I went to my butcher at Safeway, who saved bones, fat, skin, and so on for me. This time he sold me a feeder rabbit. Usually Misty would play with the feeder rabbit for a few days and then eat it. Not this one. She made it last until the next thaw, when I threw the grungy and decaying thing out.

On another occasion, my butcher had saved a five-pound chunk of a leg of mutton, with fat, skin, and plenty of sheep odor, for Misty. This was a truly novel food item for her, and I couldn't wait to give it to her. As I was cleaning the old feed area, Misty came up to the bars to investigate. I brought her treat over to the fence so that she could smell it. She breathed deeply, in through her nose and out through her mouth, as was normal when she was gathering information. She took a few steps back, her eyes began to move rapidly, and she spun around several times, as if deciding which way to go to. Her balance was off, and she ran unsteadily down the path, looking behind her as if she were being chased by something frightening. At the front of the exhibit, she stepped onto the pacing path in front of the west viewing windows and frantically paced back and forth at a running gait. She made up to seven rotations a minute, travelling at an average of four miles per hour. Every five to ten minutes, she would break away from the path and run to the back of the pool. She would dive in and drink water while swimming across to the front of the pool, where she would leap out onto the pool wall, jump down eight feet into the woodchips on the other side, then race to the front pacing path to continue her marathon.

It was devastating to watch her go through this. But it was also the only time I had been able to watch the onset of an episode and be fairly certain about the precursor. I found I could sometimes predict an onset. Misty would become nervous, confused, and unable to focus on simple problem-solving activities such as knocking the treats out of a puzzle feeder. She would sometimes act as if she didn't know me. While she was asleep, her breathing could be quick and shallow, and a paw or some other body part would twitch persistently. She stopped nest building, slapping frozen rabbits around, and other activities that normally gave her so much pleasure for one or several days until this thing had passed. Misty, a fastidiously neat and clean bear, who took the trouble of knocking dirt off her feet before entering her den, now made bad choices, such as lying in feces or food, uncaring or unaware.

Normal activities, such as getting up from a lying position, walking, eating, drinking, or investigating something, might be interrupted by less manic, more classic seizure symptoms when Misty would stand, sit, or lie still, eyes blinking steadily, slowly. Eventually her eyes were fully open, and you got the impression that she was staring into space, unaware of her surroundings. Sometimes this could be followed by a series of slow, gentle head bobs. Head-bobbing and eye-blinking episodes usually occurred serially throughout the day. I would gently call her name but receive no response.

Misty was prescribed an anti-epileptic drug, to be taken twice daily. Fortunately, it came in a cherry-flavored liquid for children. The syrup was sweet, but she would not lick it off a wooden spoon, so I had to hide it in an ice cream slurry, which she lapped up every time, except during a seizure. I made the slurry in an old aluminum feeding dish that just fit under the bear gate, so I could easily slip it to Misty, and she could quickly slurp up the concoction while I watched. The problem was that I wanted my dish back. If she spent too much time with it, she would likely turn it into a metal Frisbee. It was the only dish I had that fit under the gate. On the first day, Misty watched intently as I struggled on all fours to maneuver a stick under the gate and behind the empty dish to push it toward me. On the second day, during the morning drug delivery, Misty ate her slurry then gave the empty dish a lax backhand, sending it sailing under the gate to me. I was astounded, but unsure that she had meant to return the dish to me.

I decided that she had accidentally knocked it under the gate while she was playing with it. I had planned to give Misty instruction that afternoon on not playing with the dish, giving me half a chance—I hoped—to retrieve it with my stick before she nailed it again. Misty lapped up her slurry and slap-shot the empty dish under the gate again. Opportunistically, I gushed, "Good girl, Misty!" ok then, this looked like an on-purpose behavior. It was also in keeping with Misty's habit of bringing me things so she could get something useful in return. Clearly, ice cream slurries were useful!

Misty did not always have perfect aim and sometimes missed getting the dish under the gate. Then she would simply walk away and I would get out my stick. If she had persistently tried to shoot the dish under the gate until she was successful, I'd have said that this was a game, but she didn't. I believed that this was a utilitarian effort to demonstrate her desire for more ice cream. If I had to give Misty her slurry outside, I would hold the dish on my side of the bars, and she would lick up the ice cream by sticking her tongue through the mesh. It was messy, but it worked. Misty ended her slurry consumption by gently pushing the empty dish toward me with a toe or two.

In August 1998, the natural habitat enclosure adjacent to the grizzly bears (Louise, Skoki, and Khutzy) became available, and we moved Misty. Although this enclosure had a smaller, pond-shaped, free-flowing pool, it had numerous other benefits. It was all natural, with trees, grasses, soil, and wildlife such as squirrels, Canada geese, and other birds coming and going. It was completely open, surrounded by four-by-six-inch mesh fencing, which allowed information-scented winds to breeze through all of the time. Again we spoke to our friends at the City of Calgary sewer department, who donated two more gently used cement culverts for another outdoor den. The enclosure was connected to the bear building via a mesh tunnel up the wildly vegetated hill next to the wooden keeper steps. Like the grizzly bears, Misty had several bedrooms, an indoor den, and an attached courtyard.

We were concerned that the move to an all-natural enclosure might be too much of an adjustment for Misty's senses, but our fears were put to rest as we watched her investigate her new terrain. Misty made a point of greeting me at the fence line wherever she was—in the building, the tunnel, the courtyard, or the perimeter of the outside enclosure. She often stood still in one place, such as the middle of the enclosure, facing the wind, and just breathed in information through her nose, exhaling spent resources through her mouth. To catch a higher wind, she stood on her hind legs, with her front paws on the mesh, and breathed in. She had spied the lions across the river, and it seemed she was matching vision to smell. The smile didn't leave her face for days, even though the juices ran from her sinuses and mouth from the workout her senses were getting.

For the first few weeks, Misty watched the squirrels and birds in her enclosure intently. Then she learned to chase them and ate some of them. She could easily catch the geese, now practicing fall flight formations, who had the misfortune of landing in her enclosure. They must have been tasty, since she ate them up and left only feathers. Apparently squirrels were just for killing, and some birds, like magpies, were annoying and to be chased out. On warm days, Misty met garter snakes soaking up the sun's rays on the warm cement floor in the tunnel on the hill and would carefully step over them. Interestingly, they didn't move in her presence, though they always moved when any human charged up or down the stairs on an errand.

Of the grizzly bears, Khutzy showed the most interest in Misty's arrival. Their two enclosures were only a hundred feet apart. Each watched the other daily for hours. Louise had shown an intense interest, initially watching and sniffing in Misty's direction for several days. She must have come to some sort of understanding because she ignored Misty after that, just as she had ignored the black bears. Skoki checked in on Misty several times a day, just to see where she was. Once he'd located her, he'd move on. Misty had noticed that the grizzlies received attention, training and treats—the same attention, training, and treats that she got—throughout the day. This did not seem to be OK. If the volunteers and I worked with the grizzlies first, Misty would huff or backhand the fencing to get our attention when she decided it was her turn. If we started with Misty, she would huff and bang the fence to protest our moving on to the grizzlies. Her competitiveness led to a few bad—but hilarious—decisions.

Ophelia Barringer, a longtime animal care volunteer, was giving Misty a carrot. She happened to recall that she had a sugar cookie in her pocket, which she pulled out. Misty eyed the cookie in competitive exuberance and, rather than swallowing the already-munched carrot bits in her mouth, spat them out to make room for the cookie.

Misty's pacing habit was now almost nonexistent. But her head-bobbing and eye-blinking seizures were becoming a daily occurrence. One day, late in the afternoon, I was coming up the stairs on the hill to check on Misty and the grizzlies before I went home. Misty was lying on her sternum like a sphinx at the back gate, staring glassy-eyed into space. I had seen this posture before many times. Her head bobbed gently up and then down, then nothing. A few seconds later, her head bobbed again. As was my habit, I sat down next to her and waited it out. Khutzy came up the hill and sat with me, sitting with Misty. This was her habit. Khutzy may have been hanging around in case I was giving out treats later, or perhaps she was there just to be there. It was quiet and oddly peaceful. You could hear birds calling, the lions having their end-of-day group roar, and as always, the west wind blowing in from the Rockies. These are the kinds of things you notice when sitting with a sick friend. Misty softly came out of her trance and looked at me, a little surprised to see me. Sometimes she smiled on an awakening, sometimes not. We were doing what we could to try to control the seizures but were not having a great deal of success.

One morning Melanie McAulay, an animal care volunteer, and I had been cleaning the back areas of Misty's enclosure. We came outside to find Misty lying against the fence on her left side. As we came closer, we could see that she was having a seizure. Her front legs were stretched out. The muscles tensed and then relaxed, tensed and then relaxed, slowly, over and over again. Then it stopped—seemingly everything stopped, including her breathing. McAuley went into the viewing bay to watch. I jumped the secondary fence and crouched down next to Misty. Still no breathing. Instinctively, I stuck my hand through the mesh and placed it on her shoulder, afraid she was dead. Misty reared up her head and grabbed my hand with her mouth. A moment passed, her stern features melted, and we looked at each other as friends do in a moment of concern.

Misty let go of my hand and laid her head back down again. McAuley and I stayed with her until she got up and walked away.

I felt surprised but greatly relieved that she was still alive. I hadn't pulled back, partly because of my training and partly because I didn't feel threatened. Misty's face looked annoyed—like the look I've seen on a female bear's face when she has just had it with her unruly cubs—but not threatening. Most remarkably, I hadn't felt Misty's teeth. Placing my hand on Misty's shoulder was a professional error, and I do not recommend it. But it happened, and in that instant it felt as if I were looking into the eyes of an old friend who was seriously ill. The eyes that looked back seemed to receive my concern. The fact that these two sets of eyes were not of the same species didn't matter. We communicated anyway.

Misty—my dear friend—died a few months later, when we ascertained that she had a series of unsolvable medical problems and that we could not give her a good quality of life. Every bear is a Misty: that smart, that caring, that remarkable.

CHAPTER 7

BEING A SPECTACLED BEAR

Melanka and Nicholas

SPECTACLED BEARS ARE tree-dwelling pineapple eaters who live in
South America. Although this description is accurate, it is also
a gross oversimplification of who spectacled bears really are.
But in the 1950s, '60s, and '70s, zookeepers had little else to go
by. The fact that spectacled bears build tree nests and enjoy
pineapples seemed incidental to their overall well-being, so
they were treated like North American black bears or grizzly
bears, which are bears that we thought we knew how to care for.
After all, a bear is a bear is a bear. Thus, the southern spectacled
bears were just as misunderstood as their polar cousins, and
they didn't take well at all to North American bear husbandry.

Spectacled bears—so named because they often have beautiful white-to-blond markings around their eyes, as if they
were wearing glasses, and on their muzzles, throat, and chest,
all of these contrasting with an otherwise dark coat—are now
called Andean bears because they inhabit the tropical Andes

mountains. The tremendously rocky, rooty, and tangled terrain of the montane cloud forest is so challenging and uninviting that spectacled bear habits were relatively unknown to research biologists until the 1970s, when Bernie Peyton began his research dedicated to the conservation of this species.[1] Other wildlife biologists followed suit and have generated enough information to allow zookeepers to build beneficial husbandry routines for their spectacled bears.

Spectacled bears live in the Andean countries, which include Venezuela, Colombia, Ecuador, Peru, and Bolivia. Individuals may periodically be found beyond those borders, north and south. These midsize bears—males range from 220 to 260 pounds on average, and females are about 50 to 70 percent of that size— are extremely adaptable and can live in high-altitude forested regions (13,800 feet above sea level) and low-altitude coastal scrub desert (only 590 feet above sea level).[2]

Andean bears are genetically endowed to tolerate a great temperature range but cannot take the cold for long, unlike North American bears, who can live through long, cold winters as long as they have the fat resources that they need to sleep through it in a den somewhere. Spectacled bears live below the snow line. Their optimum habitat is the cloud forest, between 5,900 and 8,900 feet above sea level, where foods such as fruits are seasonally available.

At higher elevations, one finds the elfin forests of moss-draped minitrees and bamboo brush, and above them are high-altitude grasslands, followed by the *páramo*—barren alpine plain. Spectacled bears are not thought to live at these cold, high altitudes, but they pass through them on their way to someplace warmer, preferably a cloud forest. They do not have furry snowshoe feet as polar bears do. They do not put on fat in one season so that they can hibernate through the next, less hospitable season as American black bears and grizzly bears do. Nor do they have thick, fuzzy undercoats with longer guard hairs to sustain them through the winter as all the North American bears do.

Spectacled bears stay active through the rainy season, which is like the winter to a black bear, searching for food.[3] The forests are so richly thick and massively leafy that one can well imagine a bear resting or eating or just staying dry under a natural vegetation umbrella. The bears sleep when it's opportune—during the day or the night or half and half—depending on the availability of food, the season, and the weather.[4]

Spectacled bears have longer front legs than back legs, a feature that enables them to climb trees. Because they are light, the bears can use the large-branched and thickly trunked trees of their habitat for almost all of their life necessities, including food, nest building, camouflage, and shelter. North American bears who live in treed habitats are generally too heavy, and the native trees too small, for the trees to withstand the weight of a full-grown adult bear. On occasion, subadult or lighter-weight adult American black bears may steal sleeping time in an old eagle's nest or some other convenient prefab crevice, but they are not considered extensive tree dwellers.

Spectacled bears will usually climb a tree to feed on fruits, such as figs, hanging on tender branches that cannot hold a bear's girth. Sitting in the sturdy junction of the tree trunk and a heavy branch, a bear will bend the smaller fruit-heavy branches toward himself, often breaking them. After the bear has eaten the fruit, he discards the branches in a pile underneath him. As stripped branches accumulate, they form a platform mat. By standing on the mat, the bear can more evenly distribute his weight in the tree to reach fruit on branches farther away. Often, nests have leafy canopies overhead that protect the bear from rain and other weather and help to keep him hidden.

Wild spectacled bears are thought to use trees as watchtowers. A bear can deftly climb up to a strategic branch and observe, for instance, when the farmers have left the corn field for the day. Then, like a shadow in the twilight, the bear can opportunistically move about the perimeter of the field, helping himself undetected to ears of corn.

These tropical bears have the shortest muzzle length and the largest zygomaticomandibularis, or chewing muscle, relative to body size of any bear species. These adaptations let them grind tough, fibrous vegetable matter, including terrestrial bromeliads like pineapples, epiphytic bromeliads growing off trees, nuts, and a myriad of other plant matter such as berries, cactus, grasses, mosses, orchid bulbs, and roots. Because they can exist on large amounts of vegetable matter, spectacled bears occupy a unique niche that allows them to successfully compete with the more carnivorous carnivores, such as leopards, that they share their habitat with.

Although spectacled bears typically spend much of their time browsing and grazing on vegetation, they are still omnivorous, occasionally making a meal of, among other prey, a rabbit, vicuña, or cow. These food choices have historically gotten them into a great deal of trouble with local ranchers. As a result, the bears have been overhunted as cattle killers and crop raiders. In addition, the cloud forest has been felled to make way for agricultural land. The resulting loss of habitat, along with overhunting, has fragmented the population into small, barely viable bits, and in 2008, the bears were Red Listed by the IUCN, International Union for the Conservation of Nature, as being vulnerable to extinction.[5] Currently, most of the research being done is triage work to help save the species. To this day, much of spectacled bears' daily life remains a mystery.

In February 1988, the year of the Calgary Winter Olympic Games, a female spectacled bear cub arrived at the Calgary Zoo from the former Soviet Union, where she had mistakenly been identified as a male and named Misha after the boy-bear mascot of the 1980 Moscow Summer Olympics. She was much younger than expected and, well, more female than expected! She was promptly classified as a female and renamed Melanka, from the Russian word for "dark," because of her striking, dark, glistening coat.

In the wild, a spectacled bear cub is forced out on her own at over eighteen months of age when her mother is entertaining courtship from adult males again. Melanka was a thirteen-month-old, frightened, ninety-pound cub who needed motherly support. She was introduced to eighteen-year-old, middle-aged Rooti, who had skillfully raised at least four cubs of her own. During the introductions, Rooti seemed amused by this little cub, played with her in mock baby-skirmishes, and let Melanka follow her around. Sometimes Rooti would exercise maternal law and flatten Melanka against the ground, without hurting her, to say, "That's enough." Melanka's behavior would be somewhat subdued until the next time she broke out into a cubbish activity frenzy, trying to solicit never-ending play from her adoptive mother.

In quieter moments, Rooti allowed Melanka to nurse. Although Rooti was not lactating, she would sit up on her haunches as Melanka nestled into her belly and suckled a teat, uttering the soft melodic neighing of a contented cub. Rooti would alternately nuzzle her with her nose or touch her head with a paw. Spectacled bears are known for their melodic humming habits, and although other bear species hum, the spectacled bear melody is by far the sweetest and most soothing that I have heard from any animal, including humans.

The Calgary Zoo was a partner in the American Zoo Association's Andean Bear Species Survival Plan, the goal of which is to learn how to properly breed and raise mentally and physically healthy bears.[6] Such knowledge is shared between North American and South American conservation facilities and is useful to rehabilitation and release programs.[7]

Rooti and Melanka lived with a twenty-seven-year-old male spectacled bear named Dick, who was extremely tolerant of Melanka and often played with her—up until breeding season set in. They lived in a canopied, fenced-in, five-hundred-square-yard natural habitat enclosure, which included a heated building housing three bedrooms and a den for cubbing. The outside enclosure included a variable number of upright tree trunks with an extensive series of arboreal pathways connecting the structures. Larry Miller, the head keeper, had constructed at least four tree nests by framing hammocks made of woven fire hose with the inner tubes of tractor tires. On the ground there was a cement pond, a stream, a boulder pile, fallen rotting tree trunks, and wild grasses.

In July, Dick began to follow Rooti around the enclosure—first outside, then inside, then back outside—courting her. Rooti was not averse to his attentions and wanted to carry on with the dance uninhibited by cub care duties. Like any cub in this position, Melanka was confused and kept getting in the way, often getting squashed between the two adult bears, who were now pairing. They chased her off with increasing intensity, finally biting her to get her to leave them alone. Other times, Melanka would just turn and gallop off if either adult even looked at her sideways. She slumped into various corners of the enclosure, trying to busy herself with sticks and pebbles, as Dick and Rooti bred together, slept together, ate together, and ignored her together. Just as it was for the grizzly bear Khutzy, this was a good life lesson for Melanka.

As the summer passed and fall waned, Rooti grew more and more intolerant of having Dick around, which signalled that she would soon start to think about building a nest in preparation for having young. As was customary in zoos, the male had to be moved away from the expectant female. Dick, accompanied by Melanka, was moved to the old-style cage structures still used as holding pens.

Although it was temporary, it was a rough transition for both of them. Dick often woofed at Melanka to make her move away from him. It seemed that what had initially been a normal personal space between the two in the larger enclosure was now too close for Dick. Melanka had her own concerns. She had smelled and seen that they had tigers for neighbors, and she paced. Visual barriers were put up so that the big cats could no longer stand and stare at little Melanka. In a few weeks, both bears had acclimated to their surroundings—Dick readjusted his personal space requirements and Melanka came to some understanding, presumably, that tigers did not have access to her enclosure. Soon the bears were back to their old antics, play-wrestling. Melanka liked living with Dick.

In May 1990, back in the large natural enclosure, Melanka and Rooti were introduced to a new, very big male bear named Fernando. Fernando followed Melanka in courtship, and within a few days, they bred. Outside of breeding season, Melanka was not so cordial. She spent most of her time in the outdoor enclosure avoiding Fernando, who chronically napped in the building. Melanka ran an occasional errand into the back and would reappear either munching on food or carrying some outside with her.

To enhance their lives, a study was done to monitor the effects of giving them enrichment. In some ways, enrichment was a success. Fernando came out of the building to take part in scatter feeds and to investigate new items such as evergreen trees and rawhide bones. Although Melanka enthusiastically spent a great deal of time searching for food items, she now found herself in a position she did not want to be in—directly competing with Fernando for resources. She doubled the time she spent pacing.[8] Melanka did not like living with Fernando.

In May 1992, Melanka was introduced to another male bear, and we hoped that this relationship would go better in the long term. Nicholas, an energy-charged, lanky three-year-old male, was bent on investigating and destroying everything in his path. He was grabby, dissected walls, banged on doors, ripped fence welds off posts, and was always in a hurry. Nicholas could focus when he had to, however. A few weeks after they were introduced, Nicholas focused on following Melanka around the enclosure in courtship behavior, which she allowed. Suddenly they were breeding—for twelve days straight—and just as suddenly, Melanka was finished. On the twelfth day, she repeatedly charged a very confused Nicholas. She did not like living with Nicholas either.

Fall became winter, and Melanka brought twigs and leaves into the building. She was nest building. Nicholas had been moved to another enclosure, and in mid-December, Melanka was given access to the cubbing den, which was filled with straw. The cubbing den—isolated from the other bedrooms—was rigged with infrared camera equipment for nonstop monitoring and taping, a thermometer in view of the camera, and a vent to move warm air out of the den if need be. A den can become too warm for a nursing female, and she can accidentally suffocate her cub by rolling over him in a fitful, uncomfortable sleep. Melanka became picky about her food and ate less and less until she stopped eating altogether.

On January 11, 1993, she repeatedly wandered outside and then back inside, arranged the straw in the nest box, and then rearranged it. Sometimes she would stop, incline on her haunches, and lick her pelvis with long, massaging strokes. In the nest box, Melanka tried to rest on her side. Her breaths were short, her sleep was interrupted, and she was fidgety and didn't seem able to get comfortable. Finally, in a sitting position, she inclined her head toward her pelvis and, licking her vaginal area, carefully scooped up a tiny, almost furless cub, smaller than a pound of butter, in the palm of her paw. She placed it in the straw and scooped up a second cub. Carefully cleaning each baby, she licked off the membrane and fluids. Then she lay down on her side and curled her body around the two babies, lifting them off the straw and into her fur to keep them warm and to help them dry off. Several hours later, she reclined on her side and brought the young up to the pair of teats adjacent to her forearms to nurse.

The keeper reduced his trips to the building to once a day, entering quietly and speaking softly to let her know he was there so that she wouldn't be startled. He gave her clean water and put down spec bear loaf, a nutritional loaf, heavy like a fruit cake and probably better tasting, baked at the Calgary Zoo specifically for nursing bear mothers, who are only comfortable coming out of their dens for a couple of minutes to defecate, urinate, and grab food to bring back into the den. The objective of the loaf is to pack many nutrients into a small, easy-to-carry nugget—sort of like a bear energy bar—since nursing bear mothers have a history of not being reliable eaters. By the end of the first week the cubs were sprawled on their backs, wiggling their legs in the air, and four weeks later they were standing unsteadily on their feet, making almost intentional movements. The cubs—later sexed as males—were vocal and active. Melanka was busy and in her element, nursing young, raking cub poop out of the nest box, running food-retrieval errands, and periodically just taking a few moments for herself outside the nest box.

For the next eighteen months, Melanka successfully raised two rambunctious, curious boy-bears, who seemed to take after their father—chewing, shredding, and destroying everything in their path. When they were four months old, Melanka brought her cubs outside for the first time and taught them, by demonstration, how to climb trees. They caught on instantly, and much to Melanka's concern climbed up and down everything, including fencing. She huffed diligently at them to come off the fence and focus on tree climbing, which they did until the next time. In the spring of 1995, at the age of one and a half years, the boys were expelled from their mother's company, as they would have been in the wild. It was again breeding season, and Melanka was entertaining Nicholas's courtship dance and ignoring the boys. They were moved to the heavily enriched natural habitat enclosure at the Queens Zoo in New York.

Melanka again became pregnant and gave birth the follow-ing December to two more males, whom she spent many months raising. These boys were moved to a six-thousand-square-yard natural habitat exhibit at the Phoenix Zoo, with climbing struc-tures, elevated nesting platforms, a pool, variegated landscaping, and an automatic misting system. Although Melanka was a completely involved mother, the job was physically taxing and it was time for a break. Next came a difficult period for both Melanka and Nicholas.

It is probably more accurate to say that bears are indepen-dent creatures, rather than solitary ones. "Solitary" implies that bears have no social skills at all or have no need for social skill, which isn't true. For instance, when bears meet at a natural feed site where food is plentiful—like a salmon spawning site—they each maintain their personal space. If one bear trespasses on another's space, an argument or negotiation, and possibly a fight so that one or both will run off, ensues. These are rules of behavior: social skills.

Clearly, bears do not have a need for such intricate social behaviors as, say, mountain gorillas, whose individuals live in very close proximity to each other and therefore must cooper-ate. Although the mature silverback male is technically in charge, loud negotiations leading to peace—or fights leading to peace—are part of their world too. In my experience as a keeper, the silverback male is in charge right up until he's not—when he shows too much violence or repeatedly makes unpopular family decisions. Then he's thumped by the females, who gang up on him. He sulks for a while and then, if he is a wise silver-back, adjusts his behavior.

Female bears spend most of their time independent of other adult bears but in a small family group. They avoid males when they have young, negotiate with males during breeding season, and are known to recognize and greet adult family members in their travels.[9] This all takes social skill. It also suggests that bears have a need to be social, to interact with other bears. It is for this reason that zoos, sanctuaries, and rehabilitation facilities try to place bears with each other, so that they are not living in isolation. This arrangement can work beautifully or not at all, depending on the individual bear's perspective. Despite repeated efforts to place Melanka and Nicholas together outside of breeding season, neither bear thrived.

By late 1999, Melanka was showing chronic, massive fur loss, and she would periodically scratch excessively. To complicate matters, the two symptoms did not always coincide. She could be scratching during or outside of a period of fur loss. She frequently paced. Melanka was a chronically shy, small bear, the size of a male rottweiler dog, whose weight fluctuated around 165 pounds. She weighed more if she was content, less if she was stressed. In comparison, Nicholas grew to become a large bear, whose weight topped off at 375 pounds. He had periodic bouts of scratching and slight fur loss. He was aggressive, angry, and distrustful toward keepers. He would slap his paws against the mesh in a keeper's face, grab at the food dish in the keeper's hands, often sending it careening to the floor, and always seemed to be starving, as he inhaled his food within minutes of receiving it. Both he and Melanka had become unresponsive to the keepers and their own environment.

We took a holistic approach to problem solving and reviewed all the components of the bears' lives.[10] We decided to separate the two. Melanka was moved to an enclosure that had been designed for panda bears. This facility offered her a 550-square-yard, outdoor, uncanopied, natural enclosure with a climbing structure, a cement pond, tree trunks, grasses, and soil. Indoors, she had two bedrooms connected by a bear hallway at the rear. Nicholas stayed in the original enclosure. Each bear could see the other by sitting up in their climbing structures. We were confident that Melanka would do better living alone, but Nicholas was a social bear, and living alone might only exacerbate his problems if we didn't improve his living conditions.

To have any understanding of their problems or to influence either bear, I first had to get to know them. That could only happen if they responded to me—which they didn't. So I started at the beginning with Melanka. She was usually in the building when I arrived in the morning and would go outside upon my arrival. The message was clear: she was avoiding me, just as she had avoided Nicholas, Fernando, and all the zookeepers. So I packed an arsenal of treats in my pockets, and our bonding sessions began.

I arrived in the morning on the first day of bonding, and predictably, she went outside. I followed her outside and called her name several times. She was sitting with her back to me and her ears turned in my direction. I tossed her grapes. She was such a timid bear that I was afraid to even draw attention to her by calling her name or saying anything. The grapes had to do the talking for me. She nosed each one and then slowly, carefully, dissected and savored it. The next morning, she hung around for a few seconds before leaving the building. I followed her outside and called her name. She turned her head and looked at me. This was huge, because she had not made eye contact with me until now. I tossed her dozens of grapes and softly gushed, telling her she was a good girl.

The day after that, she stayed inside when I arrived. I called her name, and she stayed and looked at me. I threw her what must have been hundreds of grapes, which she slowly, suspiciously ate, frequently giving me sideways glances. Although I had a slate full of other work to do, I sat on the floor with her as she ate, periodically telling her she was a good girl. Over two weeks' time, Melanka would come over when I asked her to, and I always had a treat. I still found her suspiciously eyeing me throughout the day, but at least we had eye contact, something to build on.

Befriending Nicholas was more challenging. When I showed up in the morning, he would wait until my face was close to the fence and then he'd slam the fence with his paws. I—and many a keeper before me—would try to push his metal food dish into the frame of the dish holder, and he would either jam its entry with his paws or somehow catch it with a nail and flip the dish. Hundreds of marble-size dog chow balls bounced onto the floor in the keeper area. The zookeeper would then clean it up and try to deliver new food. In my book, Nicholas had every right to be angry; we weren't meeting his needs. But to better his life, we had to be able to work closely with him, and it was simply too dangerous to work with a grabby, angry bear. To stop this behavior in a positive way, Nicholas had to learn basic cause and effect. This was the school of tough love.

On the first day of behavior modification, I brought him his food dish. He punched the fence at my head. I pretended to ignore this, but my insides were pumping adrenaline. I "accidentally" placed the dish too close to the fence, fishing for aggressive behavior, and was immediately rewarded. Nicholas deftly hooked the dish with a nail through the mesh and sent it flying, raining chow everywhere. I stood still, acted sad about the spill, and left the building. Nicholas was surprised by my response and ran feverishly after me huffing—talking—to me and banging the fence to get my attention. I felt sorry for him; I knew I'd be back in an hour to try again, but he didn't know that. He just knew that this idiot keeper didn't respond like she was supposed to, and now he had no breakfast.

An hour later, I returned with another metal dish of food. I was bright and cheerful. Nicholas seemed hungry, confused, and really annoyed. He punched the fence at my head. I ignored it. My adrenaline pumped. I ignored that too. I tried again to put the dish into the holder, and again he caught it with his nail and flipped it. New chow scattered with the old on the floor. Walking was getting crunchy. I looked sadly at the chow on the floor and left the building. Nicholas raced outside after me; his huffing and banging had now escalated to jaw snapping, and the spit flew. I left the chow on the floor to illustrate what had happened: that the chow was on the floor, not in his belly.

By about 9:30 AM, Nicholas still hadn't had breakfast. I returned with another metal dish of chow. This time Nicholas seemed to have noticed a pattern in my behavior, and he had a plan. He didn't punch me in the head. My adrenaline pumped anyway. He stood next to the holder in the fence and watched as I slid in the dish and secured it. Once he knew that breakfast was on his side of the fence, he immediately punched the fence at my head and huffed. I ignored it. He followed me outside, slamming the fence and huffing as we walked. I ignored it, thrilled that he had let me place the dish. We were making progress.

In her book *Don't Shoot the Dog*, renowned behaviorist Karen Pryor discusses the learning process that helps to shape or change behavior. It takes three repetitions for animals, including humans, to understand a change and shape their behavior accordingly. The first time they see a change, they believe it could be a fluke. The second time they experience the change, they see a pattern. The third time, they test the change.[11] In one day—in three repeats—Nicholas knew that I would not replace the food dish immediately. And he was very annoyed. He didn't let go of his control over human behavior easily and tested my resolve for the next two weeks. It was gruelling—never have I been slammed at and woofed at and had to sweep up so much chow in such a short period of time. But it was OK, because in that time, I had a chance to bring things into his life that he cared about, to help soothe his anger and hurt.

In many ways, Nicky was easy to please, and he responded to almost everything we did. Instead of presenting all of his food to him in a dish, we would only dish-feed him first thing in the morning, when it seemed imperative to satiate him immediately so that he could focus on other things. We scattered the rest of his food in the outside enclosure, hid it, or placed it in puzzle feeders. We added scent trails for him using spices, perfumes, and gently used straw from other species of interest, particularly hoofed critters. Like the polar bears and grizzly bears, he received cardboard boxes and brown paper bags full of straw hiding small items like peanuts and pumpkin seeds, as well as rotting logs to shred for bugs. We increased the variety of fruits and vegetables from only apples and carrots to more than forty kinds of vegetation, including bananas, guavas, melons of all sorts, persimmons, pomegranates, eggplants, yams, potatoes, corn, papayas, willow and poplar boughs, lemon grass, ginger root, dates, and best of all, pineapples.

Anger left behind, Nicholas would now spring out of the building to see what had been left for him. He would do a quick reconnaissance trip, taking bites of some of his favorite foods as he searched and took note. If he spied a whole pineapple, he would break into a floppy run, grab it in his mouth, and race up the tree to his nest more than twenty-five feet off the ground. There, he would sit back on his haunches, broadly smiling, and meticulously pluck off each crown leaf, one by one, and throw it overboard. Then he would dissect individual juicy fruitlets from the pineapple body, slowly licking and savoring the flesh and spitting out the woody skin. The process took hours. Juice dripping from his muzzle and paws, Nicholas would hum a tune, usually alternating between two notes, sometimes gently rocking his upper body while working away. His serenade to good and juicy fruit would begin softly and then gain in amplitude and volume. Dozens of visitors from around the area were drawn to the enclosure seeking the singer, and would finally look up to see this giant and gentle bear working at something in his nest and producing a truly joyful noise. I would sometimes ask a volunteer to stay behind and explain to the public that Nicholas was busy with a pineapple, which they couldn't see, in the nest.

Nicky's attraction to and affinity for pineapples—the enormous pleasure that he derived from preparing and eating the fruit—confirmed for me that natural history information had to be incorporated into husbandry routines. Today this is called behavior-based husbandry and is being practiced more and more in captivity. Although I have seen other species of bears eating a pineapple—Skoki, being a grizzly with a giant mouth, could matter-of-factly extinguish one in under three minutes, leaves and all, and then motor on to the next thing—I have never seen another living creature so enraptured by a pineapple. There has to be a genetic encoding that attracts you to at least some of the food in your natural habitat. Species develop morphological features to use certain aspects of their inherited niche on which their survival depends. For example, a polar bear's sleek torpedo shape allows him to dive and swim with ease. It would make sense that individuals also have some inborn information to help them to recognize the plants they are born to eat, with or without a mother's teaching. Just as domestic cats are drawn to small prey, is the giant panda drawn to bamboo, or the spectacled bear to bromeliads?

Nicholas would also do his floppy, joyful gallop toward me if I was tossing fistfuls of mealworms or crickets into his enclosure. He could move about for hours ferreting out bugs and uttering quiet grunts every four or five seconds, in effect talking to himself.

Melanka also ate pineapple, but she was a small bear and rarely consumed the entire multifruit. She was utilitarian in her preparation, pulling off leaves and spitting out woody skins, and there was no song. It seemed she would just as readily eat any other sweet fruit as she would pineapple. She would, however, come galloping for whole, fresh herring and slowly skin and consume them with soft little grunts of satisfaction. Food was of interest to her, but it wasn't what caused her to express her greatest joy.

Melanka was a master nest builder, surpassing even Misty in her artistry and effort. She tended to spend most of her outside time on her highest tree platform, awake.[12] Thinking that she might appreciate some nesting material up there, I'd make the arduous—for a human—climb to the top with flakes of straw, which she would unceremoniously stomp on and toss down to the ground, making curt little grunts of dissatisfaction under a pointy upper lip. Well, that was wrong, so I stopped doing it.

Perhaps she wasn't nesting up there, but pulling sentry duty. She spent hours watching animal and human activity from her treetop, in particular keeping her eye on the multiton male elephant in his enclosure adjacent to hers, about eight hundred feet away. On occasion, she could see Nicholas in his tree nest; unlike Melanka, he would sleep anywhere. Only once did we observe her drawing attention to herself on the platform. It was breeding season, and she was jumping up and down at the highest point of her climbing structure, huffing to get Nicky's attention.[13]

Melanka's real joy was in nest building. As with the polar bears, I had initially placed the straw just inside the door in a bale, and she could move it to wherever she wanted to nest. Melanka carefully brought all of it—sometimes by mouth, other times by meticulously raking it—into the back hall. There, she spent hours fluffing, poofing, and fussing with it until the pile was past her nose and only her eyes and the top of her head were visible. She sang softly as she worked—like Nicholas, generally alternating between two notes. The volunteers, whom she knew well, and I were welcome to sit on the keeper hall floor and watch her, as long as we were silent and still and kept to ourselves. Often she also talked to herself. Instead of singing, she would utter soft, sweet grunts every five to ten seconds, lost in her work, with a wee smile on her lips.

One day, I gave Melanka about eight feet of burlap to work with. This turned out to be a huge success. Melanka set up her own daily nest maintenance routine, which always took place just before her late-afternoon nap. She would chuck the burlap aside and fluff the straw to its highest potential—kind of like beating egg whites to their fluffiest—and then turn her attention to the burlap. In a truly unbelievable display, this little bear would secure a corner of the burlap in her mouth, stand up on her hind legs, and begin to swing her head in a figure eight. Within a few rounds, the burlap would be swinging too, sometimes in a complete figure eight, depending on the length of the burlap and her gusto. She was beautiful, like a small Olympic gymnast performing a rhythmic floor routine. When she wanted clean burlap, she often dropped the old stuff in a pile away from her nest, usually in the front room, where I could find it. I don't know if this was intentional, but I have learned that very few things with bears are accidental.

Like many—not all, but many—males I have worked with, Nicholas was utilitarian and fickle in his nest building. I had to be careful to put the fresh straw bale a fair distance from the door, because he could just as easily fall asleep on top of the quickly flattened bale, blocking the entrance so that I couldn't get the door open, as he could drag it to another location.

Both bears flourished as we showered them with enrichment, offering them choice and variation. When we hit on favorite items, like pineapples and burlap, they were incorporated into the husbandry routine. Both bears stopped pacing, their fur grew back, and they lost weight and developed muscle as their activity levels increased. Nicholas solicited bonding sessions whenever I was in the vicinity by doing behaviors I normally asked for, such as sitting down or showing me his left or right paw. I made a point of spending time with him throughout the day, even if it was just two minutes on the fly to give him verbal praise.

Remarkably, Melanka was now outgoing and asked for attention from either the volunteers or me. She was particularly fond of one caregiver, Melanie McAuley. If McAuley walked through the door or up to the fence, Melanka immediately dropped what she was doing—she even let food drop out of her mouth—to go over to greet her. She would sit and intently stare into McAuley's eyes. I quickly capitalized on this bond and asked McAuley to feed Melanka her fish loaded with deworming medication, which she repeatedly refused to take from me. No problem; Melanka quietly ate the fish as McAuley stuck them, nose first, through the mesh.

In February 2000, two Vietnamese fishing cats moved into the building. Their enclosure was down the hall from Melanka, and although they were small—fifteen to twenty-five pounds— they smelled big, and this greatly concerned Melanka. She couldn't see them, but she could smell them. Their scent was as pungent as that of an adult tiger. Melanka didn't care for cats, and she paced at top speed. Nothing I did could make her stop. She tramped on her favorite enrichment and foods and ignored her nest. I reasoned that she might like to take her anxiety out on something. The problem was that nothing nonliving would get her attention. It had to be living to make an impression.

I filled up a garden pond liner with water, released eight goldfish into the pond, then gave Melanka access. She came back out into the front bedroom and resumed her frantic pacing on her preferred path, catching glimpses of the pond liner on her turns. I waited; Melanka paced. After about five minutes, she stopped pacing, moved over to the pond, and stood motionless, staring at the goldfish, who were busy swimming around. It was working.

I waited for her to plunge into the pool after them or to aggressively paw at them. It was quiet. Melanka was still. I had probably stopped breathing. A couple of minutes passed. The goldfish stopped moving. Melanka raised her paw and gently touched the top of the water, creating ripples. The fish moved again. Melanka sat down, made herself comfortable, and watched them. After several more minutes, the fish stopped moving. Again Melanka gently touched the water's surface and made ripples. Again the fish moved. As I sat there, stunned, it dawned on me that I had better find some fish food, because apparently these fish were here to stay.

It was after hours. The commissary was closed. Tomorrow first thing I would get some fish food, if the fish lived that long. For now, I had bread, which I ripped into chunks and tossed into the pond through the fence. Melanka watched as the little fish swam to the surface and took bites. Then gently she leaned forward, ate all the soggy bread bits, and went down the hall to crash in her nest. I guessed the fish could stay, but they weren't allowed to eat anything! I secretly fed them on the side.

In the morning, much to my amazement, the fish were still alive, and I secured some fish food. The goldfish became part of the husbandry routine. First I caught the fish, dumped and refilled the pond liner, put the fish back, fed them, and gave them some greenery. Then I cleaned and enriched Melanka's rooms. When I gave her access to them, she always checked on the fish first, before investigating the rest of the rooms. Every day she would sit by the pond and watch them. If they stopped moving, she would touch the water to make it ripple, and they would move again. To this day I don't see a difference between Melanka's interest in her fish and humans keeping fish as pets.

CHAPTER 8

RAISING MIGGY— RAISING ME

Learning Lessons from a Cub

SHE WAS AN angry little whirligig of desperate energy, begging for attention as she repeatedly mauled and bit my legs and hands. Miggy, as she was later called, was a nine-month-old female American black bear cub who weighed too little and ran amuck too much. Completely out of control, she ricocheted around the quarantine enclosure like a pinball. We had been preparing for her arrival at the Detroit Zoo (where I now worked), and now, with hands bleeding, legs just moments way from developing a few impressive, technicolor bruises, I was seriously concerned about her behavioral rehabilitation.

It was November 2002, and since Miggy was so small, we thought that she was born in February or very early March. We knew that she was born in the wilds of middle Michigan near Gladwin, about 110 miles north of Lansing. She was found in May by two residents as a tiny three-pound cub with a muzzle full of porcupine quills, two of which were lodged in her tongue. The residents contacted the Michigan Department of Natural Resources, which in turn took her to a local veterinarian. The quills were removed, but the little bear's throat swelled to the point of constriction, a severe complication that almost killed her. The dogged veterinary staff were able to overcome this, too, and restored Miggy's health. Within a week, she weighed five pounds. Now that the crisis was over, the question remained of what to do with her.

According to media reports, the Michigan Department of Natural Resources would have tried to find her a wild foster mother—which had previously been done successfully[1]—but Miggy was born late in the season, and no lactating female was available for her, so she was given to a small zoo facility for temporary care until room at a larger facility that could keep her into adulthood could be found. In a perfect world, Miggy should have been handed over to a bear rehabilitator in either Michigan or one of the surrounding states, then released back into the Gladwin area for winter denning or spring release. By the time we received her at the Detroit Zoo, she was too habituated to humans, and it was too late.

Miggy had spent seven months housed in a small, barren, cement pit enclosure, on display to a noisy public, alone. The facility did not have enough staff to spend the time with this sentient little critter that her developing brain so desperately needed. Not surprisingly, Miggy exhibited a full-blown stereotypy. She motored anxiously back and forth, pacing for most of the day if we left her to her own devices, which we did not intend to do.

For health reasons, she first had to be quarantined for thirty days in the animal hospital holding area. There, we set up an enclosure for her that allowed her to be indoors or outdoors. It wasn't optimal, but it did give us an opportunity to assess her development thus far and identify her needs. The floor was cement—it was a hospital—so we built her a giant sandbox three feet deep and five feet square, filled it with woodchips, and placed it inside, along with straw bales and a few logs for climbing. Outside, we constructed a canopied nest box, which stood five feet off the ground, with a two-foot lip so that it could hold a fluffed-up bale of straw. We also created a jungle of activities, including suspended tires and buckets and logs for climbing. To give her some privacy from staff members coming and going, we secured burlap to the fencing.

None of this mattered. Miggy was completely confused and anxiety-ridden and paced relentlessly. I simply couldn't get her attention. She needed an anchor, something to give her day— her life—some structure. She needed a mother, a mother to touch her, to teach her, to play and stay with her. Instead she got me, an adoptive mom of a different species who had limited knowledge of what it took to grow up to be a bear.

She was obviously weaned—which generally happens between five and eight months—and didn't need a mother's milk, but she did need the attachment, the socializing. I reasoned that a poor imitation of a bear mother might be better than none at all. I sat down cross-legged on the floor with a dish of sliced apples and slowly rocked back and forth, quietly humming a single note. It worked instantly. She stopped pacing, ran over, plunked herself in my lap, and let me hand-feed her apple bits. For the first time since she had arrived, she was relaxed and uttering the soft, guttural neighing of a contented cub.

One thing I have learned about bears beyond any doubt is that they recognize what they need when they see it and take full advantage of it. For the next three days, Miggy took advantage of the motherish bonding opportunity that I offered her six or seven times throughout the day. Then, on the fourth day, she bit me and rushed the bowl of apples. It was a coup. She had gotten what she needed from the lap sitting and had taken control of her own food. She flipped the bowl, ate the apple pieces off the ground, and looked at me out of the corner of her eye as she munched—grinning. This action became her modus operandi. When she was done with something and it was time to move on, she bit me to make me stop doing whatever I was doing. Then she would demonstrate the bear way of doing it. It was an effective behavior modification of *my* actions. Annoyed, hurting, and sometimes bleeding, I stopped what I was doing to watch her.

The "stop doing that and watch me" bite was different from all the other nipping, mouthing, and gnawing on me that she did. It was usually preceded by one or two short, whiny grunts, the baby-bear pointy upper lip of dissatisfaction, and then a definitive, lightning-quick intentional bite, forceful enough to be painful. Invariably, I yelped in pain.

The problem wasn't just that Miggy was motherless; she also didn't have any siblings. Brother and sister cubs playing together and keeping company challenge each other constantly, forcing each to test and hone all the excellent bear survival information they were born with. If you already know the best moves to defend yourself against your crazed brother who keeps bouncing off your head, then you also have an arsenal of defense—or attack—strategies at your disposal when you are faced with a similar, less-friendly scenario with an unknown animal. So I wasn't just a stand-in mother; I was also a stand-in sibling, to be endlessly abused and wrestled with.

American black bear rehabilitators often report that orphaned cubs seem to mature faster than mothered cubs.[2] Rehabilitated and released cubs have a wild survival rate analogous to that of mothered cubs in the wild,[3] suggesting that black bear cubs are born with enough knowledge to survive on their own even if they can't spend the whole first eighteen months of their lives with their mother. At eighteen months, they are usually driven away from their mother because she is interested in finding a mate again. But Miggy and I weren't in the wild, and the captive environment at the very least required some getting used to. Someone had to show her the ropes.

Miggy didn't seem to be sleeping much, and despite other choices of beds, she would crash haphazardly on the cement floor, exhausted. I tried to demonstrate all the possible uses of the elevated nest box by climbing into it and sitting with her. Although she had not gone there herself, she happily bounced after me, shredding the soles of my boots as we climbed. I did a little nest building—adjusting the straw—and then curled up and pretend-slept. Instantly, Miggy attacked my hair, trying to rip the ponytail out of my head. OK, that didn't work well! Next I tried to get us into the habit of napping in the woodchip box inside. Again Miggy followed me in, but wrestling in the woodchips was way more fun than napping. So that wasn't working for sleep, either. I had left a straw nest on the cement floor for her, and she raced through it at top speed—her only speed—going to and from someplace else. When wild cubs are sleeping in a nest, they are with their mother and, usually, siblings. It occurred to me that Miggy might still be young enough to need something furry to sleep with.

I bought an enormous, almost three-foot-long, ridiculously cushy, faux-fur teddy bear with felt eyes and an embroidered nose. I didn't have high hopes for this strategy, but I was desperate enough to try anything. When I presented the bear to Miggy, she lunged at it, grabbed it, dragged it all over the cement floor—swabbing decks—in a dead heat, trampled over my feet, crashed into my legs as if I were a tree, and finally flung it in my face (one reason that I never wore my glasses when I was with her). In less than three minutes, the teddy bear was wet and filthy and had only one and a half eyes. OK, then, that didn't seem promising either. Since she was absorbed in what I assumed would soon escalate into plush-toy dismemberment, I went to have a coffee and mull over the initial problem: getting her to rest.

Twenty minutes later, I returned and couldn't find Miggy inside or out. Looking up, I saw a faux-fur foot sticking out of the elevated nest box straw and a small paw draped over it. Miggy was sleeping on top of her bear toy. I suspect the faux fur and, possibly, the shape of the toy were the attractants. I was quietly thrilled.

Miggy dragged her stuffed bear around with her to all of her sleeping sites, and she always seemed to know where it was. After a couple of weeks, it was smelly and in need of some mending. After cleaning the enclosure—a task that Miggy always helped with by dissecting the broom, perforating the garden hose, and racing through litter piles—I picked up the disgusting toy and brought it with me to the door. As I walked, Miggy followed me and repeatedly bounced her front legs off my rear, almost knocking me over at times. I thought she was play-wrestling, since every moment is a good play-wrestling moment. She persisted and repeated whiny grunts, interspersed with more guttural growly noises, all of which I misinterpreted. I said, "Miggy, no more"—my instruction for no more play, no more biting hard, no more grabbing the hose, whatever. She ran in front of me, blocked my exit to the door, and grabbed at the bear with her teeth, but I was determined to clean this thing and held on. Miggy hung onto my belt with one paw as she balanced on her hind legs and gently bit into her other, raised paw. Finally I understood: *This hurts.* So I gave her back the toy, realizing I'd have to take it for cleaning when she wasn't looking.

When Miggy arrived at the zoo, she was a picky eater. In his groundbreaking book *Walking with Bears*, Terry DeBruyn describes firsthand accounts of American black bear mothers spending a great deal of time escorting their cubs through the bush, introducing them to new foods.[4] A mother may take her cubs to a bramble bush and pick and eat the berries, dropping some to the ground. Her cubs watch intently, sniffing, mouthing, and licking—testing the berries, leaves, and sticks. Even though they have just seen it with their eyes, they either do a smell check of their mother's breath or try to cram their noses into her mouth. The learning logic seems to be: *Mother's mouth smells like bramble berries, not leaves or sticks, and bramble berries on the bush or ground smell like bramble berries; therefore mother eats bramble berries and so I'll try bramble berries, since Mother didn't croak from the experience.* The cub may need to check the data several times before the concept is branded into memory and becomes second nature, or a given: *I eat bramble berries!*

I created opportunities for food identification and preparation lessons, bringing Miggy three or four items at a time. Like two little foodies sharing epicurean tips, we sat over a small pile of nature's bounty. I demonstrated while Miggy watched attentively. For one sitting, I brought a couple of apricots, some peanuts and raisins, and a bunch of mealworms. Gently, I ripped the apricot open with my mouth and fingers and showed her the pit inside. She looked, sniffed, and gently tongue-touched it. I put the whole apricot in my mouth—turns out that's hard—and did an open mouth chew, then gently let the pit drop off my lips onto the floor in front of her. Miggy looked, sniffed and licked the pit, then reached up to smell my breath. She carefully ate her apricot, looking intently at me while she pushed the pit out of her mouth and dropped it in front of me. I smiled—*Nice work*. Next, I took a whole peanut with the shell and put it in my mouth, where I somehow managed to shell it—turns out that's harder—and then gently lip-dropped the shell on the floor in front of Miggy. She sniffed it, lip-checked it (touched it with her very tactile bear lips), tongue-checked it for a second (placing her tongue on it for a split second), and smell-checked my mouth. The raisin demo was easy; I just had to eat those outright. Miggy smelled my breath and licked the raisins up off the floor.

Mealworms were a problem. I tossed them onto the floor, since I really didn't want to demonstrate eating them. They caught her attention immediately as they wiggled, and (thankfully) she picked them up a couple at a time with her tongue. She also ate live crickets without my personal demonstration. I am guessing that the fact that they moved was enticing enough without reassurance from me. That's really the beauty of being a sentient, opportunistic bear: there is more than one way of learning.

Most likely, over time, Miggy would have tested most of the food items that we gave her. So why go to all the trouble of show and tell? Because she needed a little primer to get started in an unfamiliar environment. And it created trust between the two of us. If I demonstrated a couple of really good natural food items, like fruits and nuts, then she would trust that it was also OK to eat mealworms. Also, I assume she had an innate expectation that her mother would take her around and show her the best current methods to harvest her food under varying environmental circumstances. Miggy paid close attention to my frequently flawed bear demonstrations. Sometimes I found her staring at me seriously as if I had just done a really stupid or "out there" thing.

It was fall, and in an attempt to meet her innate, seasonal food expectations, I—assisted by a dozen steadfast docents—collected acorns and berries and brought in bags of dried fruits for her to eat. Adult bears crack nuts with their molars. Because I was unwilling to risk my molars, I had a problem. How did I show Miggy that there was something edible inside the shell? A nutcracker was a little too mechanical. So I grabbed a rock the size of my fist. Sitting together with Miggy, I smashed nuts on the floor and demonstrated crunching meaty bits of nuts open-mouthed. Miggy sniffed, tongue-tested, checked my breath, taste-tested, and finally ate. She loved nuts, and this became our daily quiet time as I rock-smashed nuts on the floor as fast as she could eat them. Periodically, one of us would grunt in satisfaction and smile. Like everything else we did, the eating session always ended up in chaotic play-wrestling.

A couple of weeks later, Miggy was quite serious and sullen during a nut-cracking session. Normally, she excitedly danced around in anticipation and jumped up as I reached for nuts in the storage containers. Today, she seemed underwhelmed and preoccupied. Clearly, something wasn't right. She sat with me as I piled the day's cache on the floor, found my rock, began to smash the nuts, and then presented her with the cracked nuts. She protested with a rhythmic, guttural growl. I stopped and looked at her. Yup, she was definitely annoyed, as she lowered her nose to stare directly into my eyes. I smiled a little and tried to sweet-talk her into a mood change. It didn't work, although her rigid body relaxed a bit. I had no idea what this was all about. Rock still in hand, I lowered my head to focus on the nuts and smashed a walnut. Like lightning she lunged forward and quick-bit my hand, hard. I yelped in pain, dropped the rock, and stared at her accusingly for clarification. Keeping her eyes focused on mine, Miggy gently picked up a walnut and pulled her lips back as she moved the walnut back to her molars and cracked it in demonstration. She dropped the bits in front of me, sat back, and looked at me, small smile under her nose. With my bruised hand bleeding slightly, I felt kind of stupid—corrected—but I was bursting with pride for her because she was cracking her own nuts the bear way. *And the student became the master.* From then on, I simply brought nuts to the sessions and kept her company as she cracked and ate.

Miggy had a sense of humor. With a broad, giveaway smile on her face, she would pretend-sniff my breath and then try to cram her entire nose into my mouth. I believe she was making fun of me—I knew where her nose had been, and I was never too keen on having it too close to my mouth. I'd sometimes inadvertently pull back a bit if she came at my face with too much gusto, even though my objective was to allow her to be herself. I knew that Miggy detected the subtle pullback, because she stopped all movement in a millisecond freeze-frame. I believe that, in that quick stop, she was assessing if she was doing any damage or if I was about to protest. If no harm was done and there were no protests, it was apparently really funny to then press the point. This behavior inevitably turned into another play-wrestling match, nutshells flung in all directions.

We play-wrestled most of the time. As Benjamin Kilham talks about in his remarkable book about American black bear cub behavior, *Among the Bears*, the sessions were often, but not always, started in the same fashion.[5] Miggy would wag her head back and forth a few times to indicate that she was about to start playing with me and would then lunge for my head, grabbing hair, hats, and earrings. Sometimes, she would purposely not give me a warning and would sneak attack from behind.

On several occasions, I had, stupidly, worn earrings in my pierced ears. The little rings were different from my ears and always changed, so, of course, they were of great interest to Miggy. The first time she grabbed one during a play attack, I gave a high-pitched yelp in pain. She immediately backed off, then cautiously returned to the ear, sniffed, manipulated it with her lips, tongue-checked it, and then outright licked it. With no harm done, we resumed our mad play session, and Miggy learned immediately to avoid the earrings, although she loved to sniff around my head. I used the Seaweed and Peony shampoo from the Body Shop, which was very fragrant, and Miggy loved to sniff it. She would inevitably mess up my hair, pull it, clean it by licking, and very gently scrape-bite my scalp with her incisors. What was so dirty, I wondered, that I needed to have my hair cleaned several times a day? Perhaps it was that seaweed-and-peony smell?

Play was hard on me, because I am not a bear. I don't have a lot of protective fur, have shorter claws, and am not keen on biting back. So I gave dressing in layers new meaning. On top of a jacket—which was on top of long-sleeved underwear, a shirt, and a hoodie—I wore a poly-filled, three-quarter-length coat to protect my arms, upper body, and rear end from bear teeth and claws. Miggy mouthed and bit everything. Although I understood that this was a large part of her development, I also felt that something should be biting back to show her that living creatures do that. A cub with a sibling understands what hurts and what doesn't very quickly, since a sibling bitten too hard is bound to bite hard right back in annoyance if the aggressor doesn't respect the initial yelp of pain. Week after week, Miggy got bigger and stronger, and the bites got stronger, too. The list of staff who had initially—desperately—wanted to care for this adorable little furball when I took a day off grew shorter and shorter as they succumbed to her endless, bitey play-wrestling sessions.

Our plan was to introduce Miggy to a real bear named Polly, a small, five-year-old Syrian brown bear who had been rescued from a cruel circus environment after public complaints led PETA (People for the Ethical Treatment of Animals) to ask the Detroit Zoo to give her a home. We did not know if Polly was able to act as a surrogate mother, but it would be extremely beneficial to both if they would interact like mother and cub—it would give them both a position and a job. If Polly showed us that she didn't view Miggy as a cub to be mothered, and the introduction didn't go well, we would separate them and then reintroduce them as equals when Miggy had grown larger and was more than eighteen months old, the age of natural dispersion. Under the circumstances, we needed to provide Miggy with as much cause-and-effect behavioral information as we could. I decided I had to bite back.

It wasn't long before Miggy and I were deeply embroiled in play-wrestling again. I was sitting in the straw nest, while Miggy stood on her hind legs, attacking my head. She flung herself over my shoulder and hard-bit my back; *eeeeow!* That hurt, big time, like getting caught in a vise—even through all of the layers. I decided this was the one bite that should get a bite back. I was pretty sure that I couldn't bite any of her main body parts without getting mauled. So I leaned forward and bit her ear. I figured it was just tender enough that I didn't have to exert a lot of pressure for the desired point to be made. Surprised, Miggy plunked back on her haunches and stared at me over a lowered nose in what seemed like a look of complete disbelief, as if to say, *Did you just bite me?* Then a broad smile came over her face. I got the impression that she was amused. My bite was funny! It was a little embarrassing, but it did work momentarily. Since I had no intention of biting harder or of trying to limit her ability to communicate meaning by biting—other than by degree—I had to be content with my old method of removing myself from the game when it got out of hand.

The quarantine period was over, and Miggy was moved to a quarter-acre natural habitat enclosure at the back end—the quiet end—of the zoo. Here she could run and run, up and down trees, logs, rocks, and me. Our wrestling sessions grew into chase-me sessions—me chasing her, her chasing me. It was great physical exercise to help her develop muscle mass. I had hoped to get Miggy to den up for a few months before we introduced her to Polly, but she didn't have enough body fat to den. She was still eating well and living life at top speed. It occurred to me that I had made a mistake.

Until now, I had sat with Miggy while she ate. Although I had demonstrated what was and wasn't edible, I had not actually eaten with her. Fearing that I was raising a diva cub who assumed that all food belonged to her, I decided that I had to eat with her. Miggy's intended adoptive mother, Polly, had spent her cubhood food deprived at the private circus. So Polly was always concerned about having enough and often woofed and fussed at the old male American black bear she lived with if he came too close to her food. Hamms, who was twice Polly's size, never seemed to be afraid of her. He was a tolerant, twenty-four-year-old bear who had been donated to the Detroit Zoo by his owner in response to public concern for Hamms's welfare. While raising Miggy, I was also working with Polly elsewhere in eating sessions, where she was rewarded with favorite treats for allowing Hamms to eat next to her. Polly was gaining weight, and I hoped she would be interested in denning when she was large enough. These sessions were progressing well but had started in turmoil and protest, just like my initial sessions with Miggy.

On the first day of Miggy's cooperative feeding lessons, she and I sat down to two piles of nuts, one in front of her and one in front of me. Miggy immediately got up to sniff and tongue-check my pile of nuts by placing the top tip of her tongue on the nuts. Then she jumped up on me with her front legs on my shoulders and sniffed and lick-checked my face, neck, and shoulders before returning to her pile. She was wearing a wee smile, so I guessed we were OK so far. I got my trusty rock out of my pocket and began to smash and eat the nuts. Miggy stopped eating and watched me for a moment, then tried to refocus on her pile by sniffing, but couldn't. She came over and very gently wedged herself into a sitting position between me—sitting cross-legged on the floor—and my pile of nuts. There wasn't quite enough room for her rear end, so she ended up partially sitting in my lap. Miggy then proceeded to crack my nuts with her molars and eat them. I quietly went over and sat down at her pile and resumed smashing and eating nuts. Immediately, Miggy was on me, smell-checking my mouth, sniffing around my head and neck, and mouthing my forearms. I got up and returned to my pile, where I continued to smash and eat nuts.

Miggy tried several times to dissuade me from eating by coming up behind me, mouthing my shoulders and forearms, and exerting greater and greater pressure as I continued about my business. On the outside, I ignored it. On the inside, I sincerely hoped that she didn't get so frustrated that she took a chunk out of my face. Oddly, Miggy ran off into the next room, making repetitive, weak little whiny grunts as she left. Within seconds, she returned on a kamikaze run and careened through my pile, scattering nuts like marbles all over the floor. I tried not to laugh and got up and smashed and ate nuts wherever they had landed.

Every day we ate nuts together, and Miggy protested less and less. To make certain that she didn't think she had to share only nuts, I also ate other foods with her, such as carrots and dried fruits. I stayed clear of mealworms, crickets, and chow and hoped that she didn't notice. One day, several weeks into co-operative feeding, Miggy left the room. I could hear her shuffling in the den room. When she returned, she dropped a mouthful of perfectly preserved omnivore chow balls onto the floor in front of me. Then she lay down on her belly, bolstered on her elbows, and demonstratively ate one piece at a time, looking up at me expectantly as she ate. I didn't know if she was sharing or making the point that chow was edible too, but whichever it was, I felt it was important to participate. So I picked out a couple of pieces with the least amount of bear saliva on them and enthusiastically ate them. Miggy was gaining weight, and so was I!

American black bear rehabilitators report that orphaned American black bear cubs know how to den up—to build a den and hibernate in it—without instruction.[6] Wild mothers likely pass on finer points, such as picking a site that won't flood during a midwinter melt. I had spent hours observing females—Louise, Misty, and Melanka, among others—build nests. I thought I might know enough to put on a convincing show that would entice Miggy to den. She would dutifully watch me rake, fluff, and huff on all fours for only minutes, then decide it was time for another wrestling session. I was only able to interest her a few times in actually sleeping; the rest of the time she would rest (but not for long) or solicit play. I wasn't keen on slowly reducing her food intake, which would mimic a natural decrease of foods in the wild and help prime her for denning, because she wasn't carrying enough weight yet. It was turning out to be a relatively warm winter, and Polly didn't seem to want to den up either, although she had gained enough weight. Miggy was growing, and it would only be a matter of time before I couldn't handle her bites. It was time for her to learn from a real bear. We decided to go ahead with her introduction to Polly.

On moving-in day, I put Miggy in the room we usually fed and played in, while we worked to bring Polly into the building in her crate. To make Polly immediately comfortable, we gave her access to the large outside enclosure. Then the introductions began. Miggy now had access to her den room, which was directly across the hall from Polly's. Depending on which gates we left open, both bears, one bear, or neither of them could have access to the shared hallway that led to the outdoor enclosure. For now, Polly had access because she needed to become familiar with the outside yard before introductions began. Through the keeper hall, Miggy still had access to her playroom and an outdoor courtyard sandwiched between the playroom and large enclosure.

Miggy was fearful; she could smell Polly, and clung to my side. This was a turn of the page for her, and possibly for Polly if she could dig up any maternal feelings. I opened the door to the courtyard, went up to the shared enclosure fence, and called Polly over. Understandably, Polly was cautious and chose to watch from a safe, twenty-yard distance. Initially, Miggy would not come into the courtyard with me and watched from behind the door, but she couldn't see Polly from there. So as to not draw unwelcome attention to her fear, I ignored her, and continued to look at Polly and talk pleasantly to her from a great distance. Miggy inched forward, hiding behind me, and, peeking out from behind my legs, saw her first real bear since she had been separated from her mother.

Although Polly was a small Syrian brown bear weighing about two hundred pounds, she was still more than twice as big as Miggy, who now weighed one hundred pounds. This point was not lost on Miggy, who immediately began what can only be described as a rubbing fest, which lasted throughout the entire introduction. Miggy stood up on her hind legs, leaned her back against me, and rubbed up and down so persistently that she sometimes lost her balance and fell over, sometimes taking me with her. My thoughts were that this behavior was designed to strengthen our bond as well as to display to Polly that Miggy was with me—the two of us together, one unit—united against Polly, if need be. What better way to do that than for me to smell like Miggy and Miggy to smell like me. If I had not allowed Miggy to do this, or had washed her scent off of my coat, she would have been left standing there facing this giant (in her eyes) bear, alone.

Although I had been working with Polly for at least a year and we had bonded, particularly during the cooperative feeding sessions, it seemed that Miggy's rubbing ruse had worked. For a couple of weeks, Polly was cautious about coming close to the fence when Miggy and I were there, even though I offered treats to both bears simultaneously. Then one morning, in a complete turnaround, Polly came running up to the fence to greet Miggy and me when I came outside to call her in for breakfast. In a week's time, both bears were playing at the fence with each other. Polly seemed amused by the little bear and spent time watching Miggy go through the motions of play-wrestling by herself and crashing into the fence exactly where Polly was. Occasionally Polly would paw the fence and huff in play or run up and down the fence in exaggerated, floppy bear motions. Every morning, I placed enrichment on both sides of the fence so that the bears had something to keep them looking busy while observing each other.

I tried to stay clear of the games, since I wanted Miggy to focus her attention on Polly. That only worked to a point. Often,

Miggy would pick on me in an overly aggressive play fight, I think to demonstrate her prowess to Polly, or because her adrenaline was pumping and she was very excited. Either way, I was a punching dummy and had to move away or ask her to get off of me. Sometimes I called a time out and moved into the building. Miggy would follow because she wasn't comfortable enough to be in the courtyard alone with Polly in the enclosure. But Miggy wouldn't go after me inside the building; instead, she would beat the tar out of the free-standing broom rack. In contrast, Polly was extremely tolerant of and patient with Miggy. But her patience could have been deceiving, because at the same time, Polly often walked stiff legged, stomping her heels into the ground and urinating as she walked. This behavior was either a way of identifying food-rich areas in the enclosure as her own or marking it for other bears to find, since, as Benjamin Kilham suggests in his book, and I agree, bears are social creatures—but at a distance.[7] When both bears seemed confident and comfortable, we gave them access to each other.

On the morning of the introduction, in February 2003, both had as much breakfast as they cared to eat, and I put down boxes and bags full of straw filled with hidden treats such as raisins, Craisins, and peanuts as well as toys such as full paper towel rolls to shred. I also scattered whole foods such as apples and melons in the outside enclosure. Miggy watched Polly go out first, and then I opened her den door so that she could choose to go out or not. It was important that Miggy understand that she did not have to take part if she didn't want to, because she had the most to lose if Polly didn't want to share her space with Miggy. I stood in Miggy's den area and watched her as she cautiously walked down the hall to the bear door. Periodically she looked over her shoulder to check on me. I smiled and tried to sound quietly reassuring and encouraging. Miggy peeked out the door and located Polly in the outside enclosure; she was busy rummaging through a lunch box. Polly had heard Miggy's gate open earlier and knew that Miggy might be on her way. Like any mature adult, Polly continued to nonchalantly appear busy while visually checking on Miggy's progress.

Miggy popped in and out of the building doorway like a little jack-in-the-box. Within two or three minutes, she was comfortable enough to rub her back on the door frame while standing on her hind legs. Then, as if the door frame were a tree, she swung her head back to pretend-bite the top of the frame— she couldn't make a real bite mark, because unlike a tree, a cement wall is not that easy to dig your teeth into. Bears often mark trees in this fashion to indicate how big they are; rubbing leaves the scent of the bear, and the mark over the bear's head shows exactly how large the bear is. So if a bear is walking through the woods and comes across a scented tree with a bite mark really high up—perhaps higher than himself—the bear knows that a very big bear also shares the neighborhood. Miggy had marked some of the trees in the enclosure this way, and when Polly arrived she smelled and lip- and tongue-checked those trees. Then she rubbed her scent into the mix and left her bite mark way above Miggy's.

Miggy scent-marked the door frame several times and moved along the back fence line, where I was. Polly had quietly moved to the front of the enclosure and, on her return to the back fence, watched Miggy intently without being obvious. They moved toward each other. Smiling slightly, Miggy stood up on her hind legs, punching air with her front paws and asking to play-wrestle. Polly, a little smile on her face, accommodated Miggy but stayed seated on her haunches. Standing up, Miggy was only slightly taller than Polly was sitting down. The introduction had gone well. Miggy and Polly played together, ate together, and slept together, but mostly play-wrestled together. It was quite a workout for Polly, who, though she was a young bear, was still an adult, not a cub with endless energy and exuberance for games. Polly was patient, gentle, and accommodating with Miggy and enjoyed the games—at least initially.

After a few days of never-ending play-wrestling, Polly seemed to tire easily and tried to take naps throughout the day. Miggy entertained herself for a few minutes, then bounced off of Polly, waking her up. Accommodating Miggy, Polly got up and played some more. I assumed that, once the novelty wore off for both bears, Polly would be able to communicate to Miggy when enough was enough. I was very, very wrong.

I had gone away for two days, and upon my return the volunteers, who made observations daily during daylight hours, beset me with their concerns. Miggy was not responding to Polly's nonaggressive requests to be left alone periodically. So Polly developed a clumsy plan that was doomed to failure and showed that she didn't have mothering in mind. Polly decided that Miggy could live inside the building and only come out when Polly wanted to play. She demonstrated this by corralling Miggy into the building and chasing her back inside whenever Miggy ventured out. Miggy was extremely unhappy with this arrangement and frequently tried to sneak out and approach Polly for play. I tried to circumvent the problem by hand-feeding treats to both bears inside and outside the building, hoping to

illustrate that all areas belonged to both. But my attempts escalated the breakdown.

Presumably now realizing that the indoors was worth having access to also, Polly responded by corralling Miggy in her
den. Miggy tried to leave, and within seconds, Polly had backed
Miggy up against the wall. Miggy was standing on her hind legs,
shaking, and urinating on herself. It was over. I shooed Polly outside and closed the door. Although she was now safe, Miggy
came up to me with a grave look on her face, stood up on her
hind legs, and gently bit into her raised paw. I got it—*This hurts.*

I really understood Polly; I hadn't been able to control Miggy,
either. My excuse was that I wasn't a bear. And Polly likely hadn't
had the opportunity to learn much from her mother before being
cruelly separated from her. What was truly remarkable was the
kindness with which Polly tried to deal with Miggy; rather than
seriously bite or kill her, Polly tried to plan a way for them to
coexist. But she didn't understand Miggy's needs as a cub.

It's not just human mothers who need time out from their
young. Once, a Siberian tiger mother picked up her ceaselessly
demanding cub and dropped him in front of me, then walked
away, picked up her meaty bone, turned her back on both me
and her now bug-eyed kid, dropped onto the floor, and gave off
a heavy sigh before beginning to chew on her treat.

After the two bears were separated, Polly got some much-
needed sleep. I might have considered giving them access to
each other again, but Miggy remained very nervous if she even
saw Polly. So we focused on Plan B. Polly was moved back to the
bear building to live with Hamms. In Polly's absence, Hamms
had denned up, and now Polly joined him in the nest. Miggy was
relieved that Polly was gone. My first clue to this was that she

stopped rubbing against me incessantly, and my second clue was that she resumed her never-ending requests to play-wrestle with me.

By May, Miggy was eighteen months old, the age of natural dispersion in the wild, and she weighed a hefty 150 pounds. It was time that she met Hamms and was reintroduced to Polly, who had been up from denning for months. We temporarily separated Polly from Hamms and introduced Miggy to Hamms first; he was very patient with Miggy and sensitive to her small size. They had one vital thing in common: they both loved to play. Being three times as big as Miggy, Hamms could sit on his haunches and let little Miggy dance around him, mouth-fencing and play-wrestling. Miggy would get worn out, and Hamms had stationary fun befitting his greater age. When he was tired, he had an uncanny and humorous ability to nap while Miggy continued to play-wrestle, rocking and rolling around his massive body.

Over time, Polly was reintroduced to Hamms and Miggy but, true to Polly's personality, she was still not good at sharing either the enclosure or Hamms with Miggy. It was obvious that Miggy had a clear memory of Polly's aggressive nature, since Miggy remained cautious around Polly. Periodically the two females would play-wrestle with each other, but individually each remained devoted to her buddy Hamms, with whom each slept and played for hours when she had the chance. Peaceful, old, massively huge Hamms became the stress release in the group. If a disagreement arose between Miggy and Polly, each could go to Hamms at some point and blow off steam by play-wrestling. Hamms was happy to comply—either awake or asleep.

CHAPTER 9

REHABILITATING BÄRLE

From Circus Bear to Polar Bear

I CROUCHED DOWN and peered through the barred end of the crate. At the opposite end sat a small female polar bear with her back to me. Expecting no response, I quietly called her name: "Bärlein," which means "little bear" in German. She turned around and came over, looking me right in the eyes; we were nose to nose. I was completely surprised by her casual response and by what I saw: she was an adult bear—nineteen years old, we estimated— with adult features, but her eyes reflected the innocence of a cub. I had never encountered this before. Adult bears have adult eyes, which reflect experience and knowledge.

We were in the middle of the FedEx warehouse at the Detroit Metropolitan Wayne County Airport, and the hangar-amplified noise of banging machinery, motorized equipment, and confusion of people doing their jobs was psychotropic—at least to me, and not in a good way. Bärle didn't seem bothered by it at all. But then, she had spent her entire adult life in what amounted to a crate in a circus environment, surrounded by incessant noise and sadly habituated to being treated like cargo. Odd as it may seem, her crate was the only place where she was safe, where no one could physically hurt her.

Bärle's rescue had begun six years earlier, in March 1996, when Ken Gigliotti, a professional photographer for the *Winnipeg Free Press* in Manitoba, a province that happens to be home to thousands of wild polar bears, was vacationing in Cozumel, Mexico, and saw seven polar bears being beaten with prods and forced to perform ridiculously demeaning tricks, like balancing on a giant ball, during a show at the now infamous Suarez Brothers Circus. Gigliotti went about questioning circus staff about the origins of the bears and was told that three of the suffering polar bears were allegedly from Manitoba.[1] When his photographs and findings were published in the newspapers, there was a global public outcry.[2] In August 2002, the provincial government of Manitoba passed the Polar Bear Protection Act.[3] But this was too late for the polar bears in the Suarez Brothers Circus, who were already far from home, being beaten daily by human predators, and being tortured by tropical heat and inhumane living conditions.

An extraordinary team of unlikely players was eventually able to expropriate the bears in a series of unlikely events. The Suarez Brothers Circus, which had ignored accusations of animal mistreatment, made a tactical error when it moved the show to Puerto Rico, a self-governing American territory where the United States Department of Agriculture (USDA) regulations for animal husbandry apply. The inner group of movers and shakers were the Detroit, Maryland, North Carolina, and Point Defiance zoos, People for the Ethical Treatment of Animals (PETA), the

Humane Society of the United States (HSUS), the Association of Zoos and Aquariums (AZA) Bear Taxon Advisory Group, FedEx, Polar Bears International (PBI),[4] the United States Congress, the USDA, and the U.S. Fish and Wildlife Service Office of Law Enforcement. On November 19, 2002, six of the polar bears were FedExed to their new zoo home destinations (the seventh bear had been moved to the Baltimore Zoo eight months before).

It was a cold and humid night in Wayne County, Michigan— perfect weather to receive a polar bear. The drop in temperature from the hundred degrees Fahrenheit that had tortured Bärle for years to the forty degree chilly night air could have accounted for a great deal of her comfort level. This was the first of many positive changes to come.

We transported Bärle to the hospital quarantine at the zoo, where she was to stay for the requisite thirty-day observation-and-treatment period. Although all of us agreed that the existing quarantine rooms were insufficient by current standards, which is why the zoo built a new animal hospital with all the bells and whistles, we also agreed that the current facility was a huge improvement for Bärle. We estimated that her circus cage had been about four feet wide and eight feet long. She had had nothing for bedding, had eaten dog food and bread, and had often gone without a constant supply of clean drinking water.

We pulled up to the hospital doors, moved Bärle's crate onto a heavy-duty gurney, and wheeled her into quarantine. Then we secured the crate to the enclosure doorway with chains and locks. Until now, Bärle had busied herself with keeping her balance as her crate was jostled around. She gave the impression of being the most patient bear I had ever worked with. Most often, bears are extremely annoyed and stressed by being confined to a crate, and they pace, head-swing, bounce to try to break the crate, slam bars, spit, growl, woof, and huff protests in your face. There had to be more to Bärle's response than patience; time would tell as we began to peel off the layers of trauma from life in the circus.

There were three consecutive rooms, with an adjoining hall at the back, in her new temporary home. In total, she was about to occupy eighty square yards of space. This was fifteen times the amount of space that she was used to.

Ultimately, Bärle would go to live at the Detroit Zoo's new Arctic Ring of Life facility. There, she would join a group of seven other adult polar bears sharing over two acres of indoor and outdoor space, which included a 13-foot-deep, 170,000-gallon saltwater pool, a 30,000-gallon freshwater pool, and a small indoor freshwater pool meant for play and bathing. This was at least 1,875 times more space than she had been used to. We ran the risk of overwhelming her with too much change all at once. Living in the quarantine for a few weeks would act as a good transition. The only times that Bärle had had more than four square yards of space in the circus was when she was performing or training to perform.

As we secured the crate to the gateway into the first quarantine room, I tried to take Bärle's mind off the events by giving her a few grapes. She cautiously took one with her lips and, staring into my eyes, promptly dropped it. I gave her another, which she gently took and ate. We had no idea whether she had ever eaten grapes before, but they were a big success. She continued to take grapes, staring into my eyes—in my opinion, trying to understand whether I was friend or foe—and ate them as fast as I could get them through the mesh.

Finally, the crate was safely secured. The poignant moment of complete freedom from the gruelling years of torturous circus life had arrived; we opened the enclosure and crate gates with great anticipation. Nothing happened; Bärle didn't move. She sat in the crate, quietly staring. The objective was for her to cross over to her new enclosure. We were all quiet—I'm sure I stopped breathing. I think we all did, not wanting to scare her more than this move and the last seventeen years already had. It was very, very quiet; I could hear the traffic outside. Finally, slowly, she took a small step out of the crate, then another and another. Each of us, entirely focused on Bärle, whispered words of encouragement: "Good girl, Bärle, good girl." She cleared the crate. She was in. Her ordeal was over. We closed the gates behind her and on her circus life forever. I breathed normally again. From this point on, the rehabilitation began.

Bärle took small, cautious steps from the front room to the back hall. Her back legs seemed unsteady, possibly from the move or from years of physical abuse. We took nothing for granted and made a note to monitor the situation. She feigned interest in a few grapes on the floor; glancing sideways down the long hall ahead of her, she locked in on the three-foot-high pile of fluffed straw so fresh you could smell it. Like a slow missile, Bärle headed right for it. She sniffed it, mouthed it, and touched it with her paw. *Has she ever had so much clean straw all to herself before?* I wondered. Cautiously, she stepped into it with one paw, then the other. Picking up speed, she crouched down on her belly, pushed her front legs behind her, and mowed through the pile on her chest, pushing with her upright back legs. She flopped sideways into the pile and rolled onto her back, feet in the air, rubbing, gyrating, a smile on her face, saliva running from her nose and mouth. She seemed to be experiencing pure pleasure. The dance of joy lasted several minutes. In a crescendo, she crashed on her left side, curled into a C shape, crammed her right paw into the straw under her head, closed her eyes, and immediately fell asleep. It was midnight. She was exhausted, and so were we. We turned on the fans that brought the cold night air inside, turned off the lights, and went home. Bärle woke up two days later.

The greatest evil bestowed on this little bear in the circus was that her senses had been overloaded and deprived all at the same time. The witch's brew of noises (tunes playing on top of each other, people and machinery vocalizing) and smells (pizza, popcorn, deep-fried hotdogs), and the bumper-car activity of people were meaningless to a bear and had to be tuned out for survival. Imagine living in a huge mall, in a perpetual Christmas-shopping aura, for seventeen years! Turning inward to mind her own bear business was a problem too, because there was absolutely nothing to do—zero relevant stimulus for a bear—nothing to investigate, no bedding for nest building, no bears to properly interact with, nothing.[5] Like a cub, she was innocent of her own abilities.

Much of Bärle's knowledge of other bears was brutal. The male polar bears, who were twice her size, were desperately aggressive toward the females.[6] These males, also whipped and prodded by their trainer, were no doubt too afraid of their human predator to go after him, so, in a sort of bear Stockholm syndrome, they unleashed their anger on the—much smaller— female bears, which included Bärle and another female, named Alaska, who was later rehabilitated at the Maryland Zoo. Although Bärle was constantly surrounded by humans and other bears, she was utterly alone.

One of the most humbling things about working with bears is coming to understand just how remarkably forgiving some of them can be. Making contact with Bärle was one of those moments. After she had slept for forty-eight hours, I began the quest to develop a relationship, which I hoped to ultimately parlay into a trusting friendship. Responding to humans in her past had been precarious, causing her pain at worst or yielding . nothing useful at the very least. I didn't know what to expect.

She had her back to me. I gently called her name: "Bärle." Nothing. I wondered if she had lost her hearing. Again I called her name. Again she ignored me. A third time, I called her name. She turned an ear in my direction; I gave her praise, tossed her grapes, and continued. I called her name again. Bärle looked at me. I tossed her masses of grapes and gushed with warm praise. Within two days—after seventeen years of abuse—I called her name, and Bärle turned toward me. I was a controlled explosion of joy—I didn't want to scare her—heaping praise on top of kudos with bunches of grapes. I called Bärle's name, and she came over!

It was unnerving: she crawled over on her elbows and knees. Bärle had spent the first few days lying down; she rarely stood or walked. Was there a medical reason? It occurred to me that, for years, she had never had to get up and walk to get anywhere, because the cage she lived in was only four square yards. It made more sense to crawl over to the edge than it did to get up. In the quarantine area, the distance from her nest over to where I stood at the fence was over ten feet. It could not have been comfortable to crawl that distance on a cement floor. Within a few days, Bärle gave up crawling for walking.

One morning during the first week, she seemed to be favoring her front left paw when she walked over to greet me. I placed my palm flat against the mesh of the fence, hoping that she would match my behavior, which some bears often do, so that I could see her paw pad. Seeing my raised hand, Bärle seemed to want to comply with something. She looked up and saw a tiny metal shelf, no bigger than her paw, used as a feeding shelf for small primates. She dutifully tried, in vain, to get up onto it. I felt sick. Obviously, a raised hand was the circus signal for her to get up onto something. Immediately I removed my hand. I felt ashamed. I had just asked Bärle to do a trick, exactly the association I didn't want her to make in her new home.

In the circus, Bärle had spent the majority of her "free" time pacing—walking three steps forward and then backing up three steps, swinging her head side to side in synchrony with her gait. The best way to make pacing stop is to not have it begin at all. Our objective was to do our best to make Bärle's new life free from reminders of the old. Since her circus training had been done entirely through negative reinforcement, we decided not to ask her to do any training for veterinary procedures until she chose to be part of the training with the other bears. That would not be for some time; Bärle had more basic things to learn first.

Just like the cub Miggy, Bärle had not tried new foods since her arrival but just ate omnivore chow sparingly—with the exception of grapes, which she ate by the pound. It was time to introduce her to the many new options, just as her mother would have done for her as a cub in the wilds of northern Manitoba, where she was thought to be from.

Bärle and I had a series of food preparation and eating sessions. I gave her some peanuts, which she ate, nut and shell. It didn't really matter to me how she ate them, but I knew that the other polar bears ate the nuts only. I proudly demonstrated the mouth peanut-shelling skills that I had been perfecting with Miggy. In short order, Bärle was cracking, isolating, and eating the nut and spitting out the shell. Actually, the spitting process took some time. At first, she just sort of pushed the rejected shell out of her mouth and let it sit on her lip, where it eventually dried up then fell off. With practice and my demonstration, she learned to spit shells with vigor.

We ate other fruits and vegetables together; some she liked and continued to eat, and others she didn't. We both agreed that raw eggplant wasn't really worth the effort. It was vital that Bärle learn how to eat raw fish, however. Whole, raw herring, capelin, and trout were diet staples for the other polar bears whom she was soon to meet. I had put small fish piles in her enclosure; she had ignored them. I poked a herring halfway through the mesh, hoping that she would take it. She sat and stared at me. When I wiggled it, she smiled, amused. I threw it in front of her, hoping she would at least sniff it. She looked at the fish as it flopped down in front of her, then she looked back at me. I had a feeling that she was waiting for the fish-eating demonstration. I just couldn't do it. I'd likely vomit, which would be counterproductive if she followed my sage foraging advice.

Perhaps if I brought her some live fish, their movement might trigger an innate bite-and-eat response. So I put eight live trout into the water in her stock tank, showing them to her as they were poured from the bucket into the tank, slipping and flopping. She was watching me, but not once did she look at the trout, not even when I gave her access to the stock tank with the fish busily swimming around. I left her with the live fish for several days, hoping that she would eat them, but each morning I counted eight fish.

Fortunately—depending on whether you have a fish, bear, or human perspective—one trout flopped onto the floor and desperately leapt into the air, creating a spectacle of activity that caught Bärle's attention. She lay down on her belly with her nose only inches away from the fish. Her eyes grew intently focused, her smile so broad it created folds like laugh lines. When the fish stopped moving, she gently touched him with her nose and reactivated his desperate death throes. She sat up and attempted to pick him up between her front paws, but the fish slipped out and flopped to the floor. Still smiling, Bärle tried again, this time successfully. She lip-checked the fish, and he wiggled. Then she tongue-checked him and delicately stripped off a piece of his skin, and mercifully—from my perspective—ate him. After that she ate her dead fish except for the head, which she always spit out with vigor.

Food was not the only thing that Bärle didn't interact with when she first arrived. Every morning, I found her enrichment items and toys untouched. Her enclosure was almost as neat and clean as it had been when I left the night before, partly because she spent a great deal of time sleeping in her straw and partly, I believe, because she wasn't used to doing anything in her down time at the circus.

This changed in a flash. By the end of two weeks, her morning enclosure was a pleasant mess of straw, feces, destroyed cardboard boxes, toys, and puzzle feeders that had been upended and experimentally thrown into the stock-tank water. She was experiencing the daylights out of everything by sniffing, touching, tossing, tasting, and destroying. As a result, an enclosure that had been large and complex enough for a timid, inexperienced bear had suddenly become too small for a now active, learning bear. We had to increase the size and, of greater importance, the complexity of her living space in a hurry. We now ran the risk that she would resume her old pacing and head-swinging behavior to fill her day.

Bärle could finish her quarantine period in isolation in the maternity wing at the Arctic Ring of Life, which gave her only slightly more space but was all new to her. She would also gain a five-foot-deep freshwater pool in one room, a straw-filled maternity den, and the sights, sounds, and smells of the other polar bears living in the compound. Bärle was anesthetized and moved. The veterinary crew made good use of this knockdown by taking blood and skin samples, cleaning her teeth, weighing her, and giving her a second checkup; the first had been in Puerto Rico before her flight. When Bärle woke, she was in the maternity wing, and for the first time since she left the circus, she could smell polar bears.

Her zeal for exploring everything in her path didn't wane. As soon as she had fully recovered from the anesthetic, we gave her access to the pool. Without hesitation, she walked down the pool stairs and submerged herself up to her nose in the cool water. She rolled and splashed and rubbed her body and face, as miniature tsunamis disappeared into the floor drains. This must have been a delicious refuge, as the bath evolved into a three-day play session with her ball and anything else that wasn't tied down. What water was left was filthy, and we cleaned and refilled the pool several times a day.

Six of the seven resident polar bears filed past the mesh door · of the pool room whenever they had a chance in order to see their new roommate. This was a convenient and safe way for Bärle to associate individual bears with smells and faces. There were two male bears: Adak, the older and smaller, and Triton, the younger and much, much larger, weighing in at over 900 pounds. He was just five years old and still growing. The rest were females: Icee, Vilma, Nikki, Jewel, and Sissy. They were large, self-possessed, tough females, all between 450 and 550 pounds and not one of them a shrinking violet. I knew we had a difficult task ahead. Our objective was to introduce the bears to each other and create a cohesive group of relaxed, comfortable individuals.

Bärle moved up to the mesh to greet the females but moved away when the males, especially Triton, passed by—for good reason. Triton was three times her weight, more like the males she had precariously lived with at the circus. Introductions would not take place until late winter or early spring 2003, when the bears were naturally in their breeding, meet-and-greet mode.

The proximity to other bears, a pool, a very private nesting area, and daily enrichment gave Bärle the next step in complexity that she needed. We had managed to create a stable, positive learning environment for Bärle.

One morning, I arrived back from several days off to find that she was pacing in the pool room. This was critical! What had made her go back to that behavior? We assessed her husbandry routine for the past days and found the only change had been the inclusion of several training sessions. One of the keepers had not understood that we were not training Bärle until she chose to take part with the other bears because it was fun and games, to keep her from making a painful association with the training she had experienced at the circus. The training sessions were stopped immediately. Within a day, Bärle recovered and the pacing stopped. It was a poignant reminder to us that the stress she had felt at the circus was just underneath the surface, and we had to be very careful with everything we did.

In contrast to what was done at the circus, we trained bears to present paws, sides, rumps, noses, eyes, and teeth so that we could assess them for health reasons without having to use an anesthetic. We used patience, food treats, and praise to reward behavior that was well done, or any reasonably close facsimile or worthwhile effort. If a bear didn't feel like training, well then, that was that—we were done, session over. The bear always had the choice of whether or not to take part, because we absolutely never used negative reinforcement. This practice put the onus on the zookeeper to make sessions fun and rewarding so that bears would want to learn with us. Bärle had no idea that there was such a thing as a positive, no-stress, free-choice training session. There was no hurry, and Bärle still had much to learn about herself, other bears, and the great outdoors.

On December 20, 2002, exactly one day after her quarantine period had concluded, Bärle went outside to feel vegetation under her feet for the first time since she was two years old. She could spend as much time as she wanted by herself to explore, learn, and enjoy the tundra enclosure, without other bears running interference. Bärle had watched the other polar bears go outside into an enclosure that she could not see, but she could inhale the wind-borne smells coming from the outdoors through the mesh of her door. Now it was her turn. We scattered volumes of food and enrichment items on the tundra and opened the door. It was entirely her choice whether to go out or stay in; it didn't matter. Well, it did matter to my coworkers and me, we so wanted her to experience the hilly acre of natural vegetation and soil, the five-foot-deep freshwater pool on the west side, the bear den facing north, the view of her surroundings, and those delicious, wind-borne smells that filled her mind with so much information. In the circus, Bärle had been brutally forced to do everything; now the choice was hers.

Inside, Bärle stood and looked through the open doorway; she breathed deeply to get her bearings. I crouched next to her and also breathed deeply, becoming aware of how inviting the scent was. After only three minutes of assessment, Bärle looked at me, a little smile under her nose, then turned and stepped outside. It was a courageous decision.

Bärle stepped slowly, carefully, onto the grass. She repeatedly picked up her front paws to look at her palm pads. The grass and soil were cool, moist, and spongy. It must have been a strange transition from cement. It was a warm winter's day—no snow. She was smiling. Bärle cautiously walked up the little hill, farther west into the enclosure, stopping often to deeply inhale through her nose and exhale through her open mouth, devouring the air. At the pool, she stopped and stared west out to the park, the trees, and the birds. A winter haze was hanging low. She was smiling. Then she turned as if to walk back, but instead threw herself to the ground, rolled over and over, onto her back with feet in the air, wiggling and rubbing soil and grasses into her fur and skin, a joyous dance that immersed her in the scents of her new home and made her part of it.

Covered in dirt, she wandered to the highest knoll on the tundra and settled in for the rest of the day like a sphinx, head held high, facing the west wind as it flooded her nostrils. Her nose was running, and she was drooling heavily; her glands had not worked this hard for years to lubricate her nares and mouth, so overstimulated by collecting information. Was this a reawakening of the bear she had been with her mother seventeen years ago in the Canadian Arctic? She picked up a twig with her lips and held it there like a keepsake, smelled and smelled and smelled the air, and smiled. I wondered if she would ever want to come inside again after experiencing her first day in natural surroundings since she was a cub. But she did; she came inside near the end of the day, collapsed in her straw bed, and slept soundly until the next morning.

CHAPTER 10

BÄRLE, TRITON, AND TALINI

Rehabilitation Comes Full Circle

FOR THE NEXT couple of months, until March, Bärle explored and got used to her outside and inside enclosures, to her caregivers, and to watching the other bears. Her greatest challenge was still ahead: meeting the bears and becoming an active part of their lives. The introduction of another bear into her living space is one of the most stressful events that a bear in captivity can experience. In the wild, bears can usually choose to interact (or not) with other bears based on environmental, familial, or safety considerations. Bärle had seven other bears to meet, two of whom were males of whom she was afraid, and for good reason: they could kill her. Adak was a small, older, somewhat annoying, vasectomized male who wanted someone—anyone—to breed and to play with. He and Triton were unrelated males, and as is normal for adult male polar bears, they were highly competitive.

Although Bärle was listed with the Association of Zoos and Aquariums Polar Bear Species Survival Plan and was therefore expected to breed, she was too inexperienced to even meet, never mind breed, with her intended mate, Triton. Triton had seen and smelled Bärle from the pack-ice enclosure, which was just across the moat from the tundra, but we hadn't allowed him to greet her through the mesh door to the maternity wing, for the simple reason that we wouldn't have been able to pry him away from her door. Triton was a bright, play-seeking young male who had absolutely no concept of the possibility of his own demise and was as unstoppable as a tank without brakes when he had an idea. Their meeting had to wait until after the breeding season.

The other five bears were females with a range of personalities from mild and reasonable to tough with unwavering, regal self-confidence. Sissy was apolitical, preferring not to get involved in others' squabbles. Icee was an agreeable, outgoing, older female who had allowed a subadult Triton to learn about mounting females, and the two played together and spent time near each other. Vilma was bossy; her attempts to take charge of everyone and everything had been repeatedly thwarted. She was loud and argumentative and only tolerated others, preferring to play ball in the pool alone. Nikki and Sissy were sisters and had each other's back. Nikki and Jewel were friends and spent time together. Jewel was not an independent thinker and chose to run with the crowd.

These bears had been together for at least two years, some longer, had learned each other's idiosyncrasies, and had developed relationships. And they were all mature adults. To make room for Bärle in this menagerie of complicated bear personalities, we had to dismantle the old group and build a new group with new dynamics favoring Bärle, the underdog. We structured two groups to meet everyone's immediate needs. Triton stayed with the two spayed females, Nikki and Jewel, who dealt with his breeding behavior by taking part, by avoiding him, or simply by sitting down. The other group was structured around Bärle. We reasoned that her ability to understand polar bear behavior was not finely honed, so she was to be introduced to Sissy, Icee, Adak, and Vilma one at a time, at two-week intervals, working up from the least aggressive to the most aggressive bear.

March 2 was a chilly spring morning with snow still on the ground. As had become her habit, Bärle brought her breakfast chow over to the gate to munch on while she waited for the door to open so she could go out. I suspect that she didn't want to miss anything. But that day was different: keepers over-loaded the tundra enclosure with scattered omnivore chow, fruits and vegetables, treat bags and boxes, scents, and ice treats; smeared peanut butter onto rocks and logs, and threw dead herring into the tundra pool. If there was tension during the introduction—and there would be—then a bear would not have to go far to find something to do while considering her next move. Bärle watched as Sissy sauntered outside after break-fast; she had been dubbed least likely to fly off the handle in a difficult moment, and we thought that, since she and Bärle were both peaceable, they would hit it off. But bears are individuals and, as with humans, there's no accounting for taste.

When Sissy was busy dissecting a treat box out on the tun-dra, I opened the door for Bärle. In support, I crouched down beside her. She looked at me, smiling slightly, hesitated for about sixty seconds, and then walked outside, head held high, breathing in the news. En route she looked to her left; Icee and Vilma—side by side like a solid wall—were standing, staring at Sissy intently from across the moat in the pack-ice enclosure. Bärle continued and then spotted Sissy, who was busy ripping open what was left of a cardboard box.

Then Bärle committed her first faux pas. In cublike fashion, smile on her face, Bärle walked right up to Sissy and tried to stick her nose into Sissy's neck. Instantly Sissy, fur standing on end, reared around to face Bärle, jaw snapping, spitting, and growling with a pointy upper lip. She jammed her head next to Bärle's head, jaw snapping and growling in Bärle's ear, and moved forward, forcing Bärle to back up several steps. Just as fast, it was over, as Sissy turned away from Bärle to return to her treats. Bärle dropped onto her chest and playfully slid over to Sissy. This was her second faux pas. Sissy ignored her. An experienced adult polar bear behaves in a guarded, reserved manner when approaching an unknown polar bear, showing peaceable gestures at a distance. Sissy's response could have been worse, but perhaps she sensed the same absence of malice on Bärle's part that I did.

Bärle feigned interest in a small pile of cereal, which ordinarily she never ate. Then she found a large branch to drag around, periodically looking over to see what Sissy was doing. Bärle wandered into the pool, swam a bit, stood upright to watch Sissy, swam a bit, got out, and rolled the water off her fur in the snow. Now she wanted to go to the south side of the tundra and had to pass by Sissy, who was still ignoring Bärle and grazing her way through enrichment items. Bärle stood still, staring at Sissy as if assessing what to do, and began to walk behind her, but then changed the plan midstream. Bärle backed up—not turning her back on Sissy—and walked around in front of her in plain sight, perhaps thinking she didn't want to startle her again. It worked; there was no commotion. Bärle made several more overtures to play, which were met with pointy-lipped, jaw-snappy responses from Sissy. Since there had not been any signs of dangerous aggression, we left them together at the end of the day. The good news was that Bärle was able to learn in the heat of the moment and change her tactics to fit the circumstances. The sad news was that Bärle was still alone; Sissy didn't like her much.

At twenty-two years old, Icee was assertive, self-assured, and wise in the ways of polar bear behavior. The only reason she had not been chosen to be the first introduction was because of her forward nature, and we weren't sure that Bärle could handle her. On March 16, Bärle met Icee. Again, we covered the tundra with enrichment items, and after breakfast, Bärle watched Icee walk outside. Bärle and Sissy waited by the door as I opened it. I assumed that Sissy would go out first, and planned to sit with Bärle offering my support until she was ready to go out. But today I was expendable, which was a good thing. Bärle squeezed past Sissy and went outside first. On the tundra, Bärle feigned interest in sniffing enrichment items, cautiously stealing sideways looks at Icee. Within minutes, Icee walked right up to Bärle with an open mouth and encased Bärle's neck in a pretend bite. This was forward. Standing her ground, Bärle moved her neck back, hesitated, and then responded in kind. They fenced playfully with open mouths around each other's heads and necks until Bärle ran in goofy, exaggerated steps and jumped into the pool. Icee stood by the pool's edge, watching as Bärle paw-slapped the water, splashing, inviting Icee to play.

After a few minutes, Icee jumped in, and the play-fighting began. Both smiling, they splashed gallons of water in each other's faces, grabbing and holding each other under, rolling and wrestling in bear hugs under the water. Sissy, who had been ignoring all of this, eventually came to life, walked over, stood by the water's edge, and stared at Icee. Icee came out of the pool, greeted Sissy by rubbing heads, and then invited her to play by plunging backward into the pool and continuing the game with Bärle. Sissy sternly refused and walked away. Eventually, Icee tired and came on shore for good. Bärle tried, unsuccessfully, to get Icee back by slapping and splashing water in Icee's direction. Finally, reluctantly, Bärle too came out.

Bärle attempted to approach Sissy, who snapped; from about ten feet Sissy lunged at Bärle, jaw snapping and huffing, spit flying in Bärle's face. When Bärle turned around to leave—a tactical error—Sissy ran forward and bit Bärle in the rump; Bärle shot forward and quickly moved away from Sissy. This last assault seemed a little over-the-top. If these three had been human girls, I would have said that Sissy was jealous that her friend Icee was playing with Bärle, the new kid on the block. Throughout the rest of the day, Icee and Bärle sparred playfully with open mouths in between taking naps and investigating enrichment items. Sissy didn't join them.

Icee's assertive behavior was good training for Bärle to meet the twenty-five-year-old, roly-poly male bear, Adak, who was no bigger than a female. He was known for his peaceable but persistent, annoyingly blunt, and less-than-skillful courtship behavior, which often sent the girls running off in the opposite direction, jaw snapping and huffing in disgust or, conversely, making him back off and cuffing him in the head. He was the perfect male for Bärle to meet after her brutal encounters with the desperately stressed and aggressive male circus bears, and he was less challenging than Vilma. So he was chosen to join the group next. Since Bärle had been able to cobble together a peaceful coexistence with two bears, we moved the introductions up to one-week intervals.

On March 23, Bärle met Adak. After breakfast, Bärle watched from the maternity wing door as Adak, then Icee and Sissy, went outside to the heavily enriched tundra. I opened the door and once again stayed with Bärle. Not surprisingly, she hesitated. Three minutes passed; she was busy rubbing her neck and shoulders extensively on the door frame. If she was passing the time while considering her options, she likely would have feigned interest in something at her feet. Passing scent from bear to wall and wall to bear is serious business, and I believe that the scent is a land marker meaning, *I belong here*—an important statement to make when faced with the prospect of meeting an unknown male. Finally, Bärle went outside. She pretended to sniff things while cautiously taking quick glances at Adak, who was busy making an impression of his own.

Adak threw himself onto his back, feet in the air, wiggling and rubbing himself in the wet grass and dirt. He came up looking more like a brown bear than a polar bear. He feigned interest in food items as he meandered toward Bärle. At about twenty feet away, Adak dropped the ruse, briskly walked right up behind Bärle, and sniffed her rump. Instantly, Bärle whirled around to face him off. They touched noses, and Bärle moved away. Undaunted, Adak followed and rolled around in the dirt some more in front of Bärle. She joined him briefly and then moved away again. Adak padded behind her. They spent the rest of the morning near each other; either they would roll in the dirt or Adak would unsuccessfully attempt to flank Bärle in his clumsy rump-sniff maneuvers. Remarkably, within a couple of hours Bärle had decided that Adak, although annoying, was harmless, and took a long nap in his presence. She spent the afternoon by herself, playing in the pool with a giant blue ball since no one else wanted to play.

Adding Vilma to the group provided the crescendo to the introductions in a way that none of us predicted. Vilma had been intently watching everyone else's business from across the moat in the pack-ice enclosure, a fact I hadn't fully appreciated until I reviewed all of the video tapes made by Tom Roy, our volunteer photographer who recorded each introduction. Vilma pops up every time in the background, watching, running, pacing, making pointy upper lips, and huffing when bears are playing together in the pool. She had had four weeks to assess the situation and develop a plan.

On March 28, it was Vilma's turn. Adding Vilma to any mix was often like tossing a bowling ball at a bunch of pins. First thing that morning, Vilma was ticked off at having been locked inside the instant she had finished her breakfast. She paced her room making guttural, cowlike vocalizations, then stood by the door, loudly exhaling thick streams of hot air and sounding like a depressurizing gas tank. Bärle watched as an annoyed Vilma briskly marched out to the enrichment-laden tundra, followed by Adak, Icee, and then Sissy. I wondered how this would play out and opened the maternity wing door for Bärle. Utterly without hesitation, she walked out to the tundra and began to explore the day's enrichment items. Vilma came right up behind her. Bärle turned to face Vilma, and they alternately sniffed each other and open-mouth fenced. They were both smiling. Vilma was her usual pushy and aggressive self. She backed Bärle up repeatedly and eventually led her down to the pool's edge. This was where Vilma's agenda became clear.

With a broad smile on her face, Vilma leapt into the pool and paw-splashed Bärle, who was still on land. What seemed both odd and humorous was that, as much as Bärle loved the water, she just stood with a smile on her face, watching. Vilma, not a patient bear, slapped the water with greater and greater vigor, using not one but both paws. Other bears, keepers, and I were now splotchy wet. But Bärle, water dripping off her brow and into her eyes, continued to stand there watching. Vilma was beyond mildly ticked off. With an overhanging pointy upper lip, she began splashing the water with her entire upper body, making huge waves of water that flew onto Bärle, keepers, and now zoo visitors. Everyone was howling with laughter except for Bärle, who had stopped smiling. She cautiously got into the water next to the aerobic Vilma, who immediately enveloped her in a hug and a tumble. Bärle reciprocated, trying to hold Vilma under water; both surfaced smiling. I suspect Bärle initially hesitated because she was sizing up Vilma's true intent. Their game was endless and was played out between friends over days, weeks, and years.

It was early July, and Triton's usual, wild and crazy, rodeo-esque breeding behaviors had finally subsided to little more than an interest. It was time to introduce him to Bärle. He was still over nine hundred pounds and about three times as large as Bärle. But Bärle had become more knowledgeable about other bears, and it emerged that she knew how to keep a cool head and reconsider strategy on the spot to accommodate and avoid aggression. She had likely honed that skill in the circus to survive the cruelty of physical punishment. So far, Bärle had managed every bear's idiosyncrasies by responding on their terms; Sissy wanted to be alone, so Bärle learned to leave her alone; Icee wanted to mouth-fence, so they mouth-fenced; Adak wanted to roll in the dirt, so they rolled in the dirt; Vilma wanted to play in the water—well, finally a bear who wanted to do something that Bärle wanted to do—so they played in the water and became friends for life. But with Triton, it was different. He was an aggressive bear but not an angry bear; in fact, he could be sweet to the point of being soulful, showing deep emotional meaning. Bärle's challenge was to get beyond her well-justified fear of these massive, foreboding males and view Triton as an individual.

After breakfast on July 11, Bärle watched as Triton, Vilma, and Icee walked past her door in the maternity wing, out to the heavily enriched tundra enclosure. We specifically chose to have Vilma and Icee at the introduction because Icee was Triton's buddy and could keep him in line. Vilma was part of Bärle's posse and would look after her interests (well, first Vilma looked after her own interests, then Bärle's). We excluded Sissy because she loathed conflict, and should this introduction erupt into aggression and disagreement, Sissy would either get in the way—by trying to get out of the way—or she would glue herself against a wall.

I opened the door for Bärle and stayed with her, trying to be encouraging and supportive. She hesitated for more than ten minutes, first busily rubbing her head and body against the door frame and then standing in the doorway, deeply inhaling the airborne information. Finally, this brave little bear stepped out. Bärle wandered up the hill and spotted Triton, then turned her back to him. This made me nervous; not being a bear, I had no idea if this was a faux pas, a tactical error, or the smartest thing she could have done.

Triton was busy eating the leaves off of the sugar maple branches—his favorite—which were part of the day's enrichment. Like Adak, he wasted no time, and purposefully ate his way closer to Bärle. Within thirty feet of her, he bounded over in an exaggerated, playful, but also aggressive (like a freight train) gait and crammed his head next to hers, vigorously sniffing her and smacking his lips. Instantly, Bärle reared up and bounced off him with her front paws, pushing him backward as she jaw snapped and growled. Icee and Vilma paid close attention to the action while feigning interest in treats. Triton continued his aggressive sniffing and attempted to flank Bärle. She stood her ground and faced him off. Triton backed up, stared at Bärle for a moment as if in thought, picked up a sugar maple branch with his mouth, and presented it to Bärle. Not only did she ignore it but she sat down to foil his rump-seeking maneuvers. Dejected, Triton backed off. According to Icee and Vilma, the worst was over, as they lowered their heads and genuinely went about their foraging business. So I relaxed a bit. Triton and Bärle both sat quietly for a few minutes, and then Bärle reopened negotiations by sliding in the grass on her belly over to Triton. Triton tried to flank her again, and she backed away.

Triton moved off again, head and upper lip hanging loose, dejected. But he had been thinking. Within minutes, he returned, dragging the entire sugar maple tree trunk in his mouth over to Bärle and plunking it down in front of her. For the first time, a broad smile came over her face—to match the broad smiles on all of our human faces—and yet Bärle continued to feign lack of interest. Again Triton picked up the tree and crashed it down in front of her. This time, Bärle accepted the gift by gently touching a branch with her lips, still smiling. Icee was now watching intently. Triton smiled, new confidence creeping into his posture as he attempted his rump-seeking maneuver again. And again, Bärle just graciously sat down—game over! But they had been successfully introduced.

Bärle was also successfully introduced to Nikki and Jewel. All eight bears had accomplished our objective of them living together peaceably. Because Triton would fight with Adak when they were together, we had to keep them separated. So we managed two groups, each with a male and whatever females seemed interested in being together with whichever male on any given day. Bärle and Triton bonded and often stayed close to each other. Icee, who had patiently allowed Triton to practice his clumsy breeding skills with her when no one else wanted to be around his annoyingly rambunctious, teenage male self, was not happy about this and tried to lure Triton away with play, or sometimes by body rubbing in coy seduction.

Regardless, breeding in the spring of 2004 was a given. Bärle got to spend exclusive time with Triton, while the other girls had to put up with Adak, who was also bitten by the breeding bug, more so this year than before—likely because Triton was now a viable breeding male to compete with from across the moat. Icee spent much of her time watching Bärle and Triton, also from across the moat.

Triton followed and wooed Bärle, and judging by the warm little smile that she constantly wore, she was utterly accepting and completely enamored. Triton even presented Bärle with a pvc puzzle feeder, still fully loaded with treats, as a gift.

Triton is not the only male polar bear who has been observed giving gifts. According to Christine Bartos of the Maryland Zoo, when Alaska—the other female polar bear rescued from the

Suarez Brothers Circus—arrived at the zoo, she too had to get to know her environment before being introduced to her new mate, Magnum. He was a young male polar bear who had lived alone for a period of time, and despite extensive enrichment programming, he paced every day. As soon as Alaska arrived in the building, his pacing stopped, and he set up his own introduction by fervently stuffing his straw bedding under the wee crack in the door separating them. The straw could have been his olfactory calling card, saying, *I'm here*; it could have been a provisional gift in case she didn't have any straw; it could have been that straw was the only gift that actually fit under the door, or it could have been a combination of all three. It was a delightful and ingenious introduction, which Alaska readily accepted by sniffing, lip-checking, and mouthing for information.

When Bärle and Triton began to show a renewed interest in the world around them as the hormone-infused fury of coupling waned, they were put back together with the other females, and Triton ran off the last of his steam with Icee, a spayed female. In the fall of 2004, Bärle quietly began to distance herself from the other bears and seemed preoccupied. She spent time investigating the maternity wing, especially the den area, arranging and rearranging straw. This was the cue for keepers to separate her from the other bears so that she had complete privacy, and Bärle denned up. On November 22, my colleague Betsie Meister, zookeeper supervisor, observed Bärle on closed-circuit television becoming progressively restless; she changed her lying positions often, got up and moved around, then slowly lay down again. At 11:08 in the evening, Bärle settled down and gave birth to a single, tiny, pinkish cub, small enough to fit into a human hand, covered with a dusting of clear fur.

Scant records indicate that Bärle was taken from the wild as a cub between one and two years of age. No one knows whether Bärle was orphaned by the accidental shooting of her mother by an unskilled or unethical hunter or on purpose, by a paid hunter to generate cubs for captivity—an extremely unethical practice, fuelled by human greed, that is less common today. In either case, Bärle was raised by her mother. As a result, she had the information she needed to raise her own young. Remarkably, after seventeen torturous circus years, Bärle was able to call up this knowledge and has become the skilled and doting mother of a female—now young adult—polar bear, named Talini. The Detroit Zoo has chronicled Bärle's gentle and intelligent cub rearing in a film, which is featured on their Web site.[1]

As Talini went through the normal cub stages of development—opening her eyes; growing thick fur; developing tiny, pin-sharp teeth; learning to walk; following her mother; showing interest in whole foods—Bärle created opportunities to teach her cub by demonstration. Most remarkably, and never previously observed in the wild or in captivity, Bärle taught Talini how to hunt seals underwater at the Detroit Zoo.

The polar bears' 170,000-gallon saltwater pool abuts the seals' 100,000-gallon pool. Their adjoining wall was constructed of massively thick acrylic windows, so the bears can see the seals, and the seals can see the bears, as they swim underwater. In the initial bear-to-seal introductions, it took most of the seals less than a few hours to understand that the polar bears could not get at them. Over time, the bears and seals became so familiar with each other that they played together, particularly Triton and an equally large male gray seal named Kiinaq (pronounced Kee-nack).

Bärle taught Talini to swim in progressively deeper pools, starting with the freshwater play pool in the maternity wing, moving to the freshwater pool in the tundra enclosure, and finally graduating to the large saltwater pool in the pack-ice enclosure. During the swimming lessons, Bärle moved farther and farther into the deep end, while Talini relentlessly tried, by splashing, doing somersaults, and otherwise goofing around, to entice her mother to come back to play in the shallow end. Eventually, Talini became a proficient swimmer and followed her mother into the deep end, closer and closer to the seal pool.

In the fall of 2005, when Talini was a yearling, the seal-hunting lessons began and went on for months. Carol Bresnay, a Detroit Zoo animal enrichment volunteer, observed a serious teaching session in which Talini floated in the water behind her mother, facing the seal window. Bärle hid behind the rock outcropping, then sprang forward toward the seal and gave chase. She repeated this maneuver over and over while Talini dutifully observed. To this day, Talini uses this technique and another one, believed to be of her own making, intermittently, depending on the hunting strategy required.

On many occasions, Carrie McIntyre, another Detroit Zoo animal enrichment volunteer, has observed Talini hunting seals the wild way—mimicking an ice floe by floating motionless in the water until the seal comes very close, when she springs to life and plays "catch me, catch me" with Kiinaq.

In raising Talini, Bärle's rehabilitation has come full circle. You cannot humanize a bear, and you cannot "debearize" a bear. Give bears what they need to carry on their bear lives, and they will, even if what it means to be a bear has lain buried for years.

WHAT BEARS NEED—
YOU AND ME

BÄRLE, TRITON, MIGGY, Misty, Snowball, Louise, Skoki, and Khutzy—
all of these bears and the rest of the bears I have worked with
are true individuals, responding to their circumstances based
on their genetics, environment, and unique experiences. Some,
like Louise and Tiny, take control of their environment, whereas
others, like Sissy and Patches, prefer to remain apolitical in their
everyday dealings. Even so, Louise controlled differently from
Tiny, and Sissy was apolitical in a different way from Patches.

The common denominator is that they are utterly convinced
of being bears; whether they are human raised or mother raised,
they make no attempt to be something else to please you. Quite
the opposite: bears have bear expectations and can become
quite indignant if you don't meet them; even young bears like
Miggy, who, using innate knowledge, frequently demonstrated

how things were to be done properly, the bear way, often biting me to get my attention for instruction.

At the same time, bears have often shown great patience in their attempts to communicate something to me. There is nothing—nothing—a human can do to a bear that will change his perception that he is a bear with bear needs. If he is a bear living in captivity, then he is a bear with a different skill set; if he is a bear who has been abused, then he is a bear suffering the bear way; if he is a bear living in the wild, then he is a bear living in the wild with a wilderness skill set and bear needs.

There are eight species of bears in the world. One species is Red Listed as endangered (the giant panda), and five are listed as vulnerable (the polar bear,[1] Andean (spectacled) bear, Asian (Himalayan) black bear, sun bear, and sloth bear) by the IUCN, International Union for Conservation of Nature.[2] Although the American black bear and the brown bear are globally listed as being of least concern,[3] both species are rapidly losing ground. The Gobi desert brown bear is the most endangered bear in the world[4]—there are only twenty to twenty-five individuals left. The Rocky Mountain grizzly bear population in Alberta has fallen below four hundred individuals and is in crisis.[5]

Bears are in trouble and need our help, but how can we give it to them? What can each of us do to make a real difference, a difference that matters directly to their survival? There are hundreds of ways to help bears locally, nationally, and internationally.

One reason it is so important to help bears is that they are an umbrella species occupying a position high on the food chain within their natural community. The best known example—widely highlighted by the media—is the polar bear, who sits at the top of the Arctic food chain as the largest land carnivore. In oversimplified terms, polar bears eat seals, seals eat fish, and fish eat plankton. Polar bears are the proverbial canary in the coal mine; if polar bear populations aren't doing well, then there is trouble farther down the food chain, too. If we save the Arctic for polar bears, we have also saved it for seals, fish, and plankton—and for arctic foxes, walruses, lemmings, snowy owls, wood frogs, and every other creature living there. Sadly, it is precisely this chain reaction that makes it difficult to save bears.

The needs of bears are so wide-ranging that they inevitably come into conflict with human interests and perceived necessities. For this reason, polar bears were only listed as threatened by the Bush Administration in the U.S. in May 2008, and are not yet listed as threatened by the Canadian government. As I write this, polar bears have no status on Environment Canada's Species at Risk list,[6] despite the fact that the Manitoba government just designated them as threatened in February 2008. The story of Alberta's grizzly bears is similar. In 2002, the Alberta Endangered Species Conservation Committee (ESCC) recommended that grizzly bears be designated by the Alberta government as threatened.[7] This has not happened, even though the population has fallen below four hundred individuals and is not thought to be self-sustaining without critical measures to keep the bears' habitat intact and protected.

The bright lights in the mist are the dedicated individuals and organizations that are intelligently and aggressively taking on global bear issues. These include the International Association for Bear Research and Management, Polar Bears International, the Aspen Valley Wildlife Sanctuary, Animals Asia, and many others. There are myriad exciting ways to get close to bears who need your help, or to help from a distance. The appendix lists other organizations that are dedicated to the conservation and welfare of bears.

The International Association for Bear Research and Management (IBA) developed their bear conservation fund in 2002 to allocate much-needed funds to wild bear research projects around the world. We cannot conserve what we do not understand or even know about. One of these fascinating projects is unfolding in South America. Robyn Appleton is a real-life Indiana Jones, and has made a discovery older and more valuable than Indy's "archeological junk."[8] Dating back some ten thousand years,[9] it is about five times older than the Temple of Doom! Robyn, a Canadian PhD candidate, has discovered desert spectacled bears—not just one or two elusive (to humans) individuals but many Andean bears—coming and going from hidden oases of vegetation and life-giving water holes in the tropical dry forest of Peru.[10] Until 2007, no one had been able to locate areas of resources frequently used by the bears. With Appleton's Peruvian expedition team member Javier Vallejos Guerrero, an exceptional local animal tracker and conservationist, Appleton and her team hiked for weeks in the forbidding desert valleys hidden by the steep, scree slopes of the foothills nestled in between the Peruvian Pacific Ocean and the western slopes of the Andean mountains. They found the bears, like a cluster of jewels in a mine, in pockets of undisturbed habitat—a complete rarity today.

There were spectacled bears and their signs—shredded trees, feces, fur, footprints, and day beds—everywhere. Robyn settled in and made preliminary behavioral observations of the desert bears as they carried on with their daily routines. Only mothers with cubs seemed slightly cautious in her presence and moved their cubs away. Appleton told me about one bear, who she suspected had never seen a human before, who was so curious that she nonchalantly came within three feet of the little cliff that Appleton was sitting on.

Small water-hole oases in the desert provide for an entire community of wildlife, including cougars, ocelots, anteaters, foxes, and skunks, who come at night to drink, and deer, who come to drink at around noon and early evening. Bears show up, too, in the late morning and early evening, to drink and bathe.[11] To conserve spectacled bears, it is vital that these oases not become an archipelago of isolated islands, separated by human roads and habitation, along the Peruvian West Coast—a process well underway in other areas. The first step toward conservation is to identify bear corridors and bear needs and to help the already inspired local communities, who were excited to discover that there were still spectacled bears on their land, build programs to protect their natural heritage through education. Appleton is as courageous as she is committed and has already given much of herself, in both effort and funding, toward the well-being of both the bears and the local communities. She has begun the next phase of her research but needs continued funding.

Dozens of exciting and vital research projects like Appleton's exist around the world, led by dedicated and dogged scientists who rely heavily on donations for an opportunity to save our bears. Anyone who wishes to support these field projects can get directly involved by donating online to the Bear Conservation Fund, created by IBA, at www.bearbiology.org. The fund gives 85 percent of the monies to field research and 15 percent for outreach. A full 100 percent benefits wild bears.

Another worthy organization is Polar Bears International, which reaches out to help polar bears wherever they are, including in captivity. Gail Hedberg, a neonatal care specialist and senior veterinary technician at the San Francisco Zoo, has been involved in rearing hundreds of baby animals, including panda bears and polar bears, at dozens of facilities.[12] Her work provides an example of how Polar Bears International has helped us understand wild polar bears and improved the lives of captive bears. As she reviewed the historical data on hand-reared polar bear cubs around the world, she found that many were susceptible to broken bones, rickets, and poor formula tolerance. Hedberg zeroed in on a dietary taurine deficiency as the possible culprit.

Taurine is vital to vitamin D absorption in the body, and vitamin D is vital to bone health. Some animals, such as dogs, can produce taurine in their bodies; other animals, such as cats, who are exclusive obligate carnivores, meaning that they must eat meat proteins to live, cannot produce taurine and must obtain it from their food. This isn't a problem for free-living carnivores, since they ingest plenty of taurine in their meat diets, but for captive animals like pet cats, taurine has to be added to their processed diets in effective quantities. No one knows if polar bears can synthesize their own taurine or if they, like obligate carnivores, get it in their wild diet.

To measure taurine levels in polar bear milk, Hedberg needed samples. Polar Bears International sponsored the research and helped to organize the acquisition of wild milk, provided by Canadian biologist Andrew Deroucher, from a Norwegian bear population, through the Norwegian Polar Institute.[13] The resulting analyses showed that wild polar bear milk contains much higher levels of taurine than previously thought,[14] suggesting that cubs being hand-raised in captivity need a taurine boost in their diets. This work provides vital information for raising mentally and physically healthy polar bears in captivity. If polar bear populations are depleted, we may well need to know how to raise healthy, strong unhabituated bears in captivity for eventual reintroduction into wild areas where the pack ice has been preserved.

THE ASPEN VALLEY Wildlife Sanctuary is hidden deep in the woods of Ontario, in what southern Ontarians call the north and northern Ontarians call the south. Invariably, whenever I go there, I get lost driving down the charmingly potholed, remote, sometimes gravel roads completely flanked by trees, bush, and lakes. While I wrote this book, one hundred rehabilitating American black bear cubs were hibernating in tree nests and ground dens in natural enclosures so large they are measured in acres, not square yards. In the spring of 2008, they were released in small groups, in remote, secret areas acting as lush, discreet launching pads for the rest of their lives. One hundred cubs—an unimaginable number—make the Aspen Valley Wildlife Sanctuary the largest bear rehabilitation facility in the world.

The sanctuary began when Audrey Tournay, a high school teacher and committed animal conservationist, bought a farm in the Parry Sound area and moved from her urban home in the Niagara region. She planted thousands of evergreens and turned much of her land back over to nature. One day in 1972, someone brought Tournay an injured raccoon: would she please look after him and nurse him back to health? Thirty-six years and thousands of healthy released wild animals later, the dedicated and utterly unsinkable Tournay is the founding director of a one-thousand-acre rehabilitation sanctuary with the staff and volunteers to work it.

By 1990, word of the sanctuary had spread, and animals were arriving on a daily basis from as far as the United States and as close as down the road. Tournay needed help. As it happened, Tony Grant, a ten-year volunteer veteran, had sold his businesses and was retiring. He offered to come up from southern Ontario to help for a few weeks until Tournay could hire someone else. Grant worked nonstop, day after day, until one day he realized that he had lived for an entire year in a trailer on the site. He bought a home in the area and made it official: he had retired into becoming the manager of the Aspen Valley Wildlife Sanctuary. Grant, an expert bear rehabilitator, estimates that in his sixteen-year run they have rehabilitated and released well over six hundred American black bears.

Each bear arrives at the sanctuary with his or her own story, each more deplorable than the last. The bear that received the most media coverage was Buddy, an abused black bear cub who was kidnapped from his mother in the fall of 2003 by a predatory human male in Wakefield, Quebec, who repeatedly ran over the swimming cub with his Jet Ski.[15] When that failed to sufficiently subdue the cub, the attacker grabbed him by a rear leg and brutally dunked him in the water repeatedly until the cub was exhausted. In a final effort to save his own life, the cub was able to make a dash for the shore but was physically tackled by the perpetrator. Ultimately, Quebec officials rescued Buddy and gave him to the Aspen Valley Wildlife Sanctuary in Ontario for rehabilitation.

Despite the public's outrage, this inhumane crime has gone unpunished. Embarrassingly, Canada's ineffective animal cruelty legislation has not been updated effectively since 1892.[16] The dedicated, expert staff at the sanctuary nurtured Buddy back to health, and the last time they saw him, his yearling rear end was bounding off toward the woods in Quebec during his release in July 2004.[17] For this rescue, and hundreds of others accomplished by this team, Tournay and Grant accepted the Animal Action Award from the International Fund for Animal Welfare in 2004 at the Parliament Buildings in Ottawa, alongside Jane Goodall, who was also an Animal Action Award winner.[18]

A FINAL, DRAMATIC example of bear rescue work comes from Asia. Asiatic black bears like Ping Pong and Lailo, Red Listed by the IUCN, are also listed in Appendix I (species in greatest peril of becoming extinct) of the Convention on International Trade in Endangered Species (CITES), making it illegal to trade internationally in their body parts.[19] Still, there are thousands of Asian black bears left on the planet—all captive, languishing in abject horror in bear bile farms in China, Vietnam, and South Korea. This utterly inhumane state of affairs began in the 1980s. Wild populations of Asian black bears were depleted by hunters looking for bear bile and bear gall bladders used in traditional Chinese medicines, and bear paws used to make bear paw soup, which can sell to culinary fashionistas for a thousand dollars a bowl. Bears are long-lived and slow to reproduce. When you kill a wild bear, it matters to the population. In a well-meant but disastrous effort to help stop wild bear poaching—it is illegal to hunt Asian black bears—the Chinese government encouraged and issued licenses to farm the bears. Hundreds of small mom-and-pop subsistence farms, each holding maybe a dozen bears, sprang out of the dirt, and numerous very large farms were built, each holding approximately three hundred bears, for what is thought to be a total of about seven thousand bears on Chinese bile farms today.

Bear bile—as well as human bile, squirrel bile, and any other animal bile—contains ursodeoxycholic acid (UDCA), the metabolic by-product of intestinal bacteria. UDCA is a much-sought-after medicinal ingredient, said to help heal high fevers, liver disease, and less-deserving ailments such as hemorrhoids and hangovers. Western medicine uses ursodiol, the synthetic reproduction of UDCA, to dissolve or prevent gallstones. In addition, a promising scientific study now reveals that the substance interferes with the continued growth of colon cancer cells, inducing cell differentiation and cell senescence.[20] Combinations of herbal formulas, tinctures, and tonics also act as medicinal replacements for bear bile. Sadly, the advent of these much less expensive alternatives actually created a fashionable demand for real bear bile among those who have the money to pay for it and consider synthetics to be cheap knockoffs.

Bear bile is now faddishly put into nonmedicinal products such as chewing gum, toothpaste, and face cream. These products also end up on the North American market despite the Asian black bears' Appendix I CITES status making international trade illegal. The bear bile issue is global: Interpol reported that its Operation Bear Net, which lasted for over four years, uncovered 786 bear gall bladders collected by Quebec hunters, trappers, and poachers and sold by three major dealers in Canada to several countries in Asia.[21]

In China, Asian black bears are held in incomprehensibly inhumane conditions in which they are reduced to living bile machines. Each bear lies down, permanently, in a coffin-shaped, wire mesh crate for his entire life—years—able to move only one arm so that he can reach out for food. Without proper anesthetic, drugged only half-unconscious, the bear is tied down by ropes, and a metal catheter, which eventually rusts, is permanently stuck through his abdomen into his gall bladder. Bile, full of pus, is tapped from the bear in daily sessions, which one can only imagine to be excruciatingly painful. Over time, some bears lose their minds and bang their heads on the bars and rub their noses in repetitive patterns to the point of rubbing off fur, skin, and finally, cartilage. Many bears die slow, agonizing deaths, as peritonitis consumes the skin of their internal organs. Many bears are declawed (the first bone of each finger is cut off), and many are also detoothed, without proper anesthetic. Each bear is rendered completely, utterly defenseless, while fully aware of his human predator, for years, until he dies.

In 1993, Jill Robinson withdrew from the rest of her tour group at a bear bile farm and slipped down a staircase leading to a darkened basement. There, she heard the clacking of a terrified bear, who had become aware that a predator was in the room. The spectacle was so unbelievable that it was difficult for her to immediately grasp as her eyes adjusted to the darkness. In her own words, she was in a "bear torture chamber." As Robinson cautiously moved closer, the bear's clacking grew faster, desperately anxious. Another, female bear stretched out her paw and touched Robinson's shoulder. Robinson turned to look and instinctively reciprocated, reaching out to the bear. Gently, repeatedly, the bear squeezed Robinson's fingers and took hold of Robinson's heart.

It's impossible to meet Jill Robinson and not be utterly awestruck by the enormity of her calling. The remarkable story of her first meeting with a tortured bear has been told and retold in the media because it set the stage for her work. I had read it, but was fortunate enough to hear Robinson tell the story at a bear care conference in 2007, where she gave the keynote address about her inspiring work to rescue bears.

In 1998, Robinson founded Animals Asia, a powerfully driven Asian animal-welfare organization whose mandate is to rescue abused bears, pets, and other animals and restore respect for animals in Asian culture—historically, animals were valued in traditional Buddhist and Confucian thought.[22] Like many other urban-centered cultures around the world, including in North America, where the cruelties of factory-farming chickens, pigs, and cattle are hidden but supported, China somehow lost its way. In the twenty-first century, China is undergoing another cultural reformation fuelled by its desire to compete in the global market. In 2000, Robinson, as CEO and founder of Animals Asia, signed a historic agreement with the Chinese government to rescue five hundred bears from bile farms, with a mutual promise to work toward ending the practice of bile farming. The Chinese government has also stopped issuing licenses for bile farms.

But what do you do with an eventual five hundred bears desperately in need of medical and psychological help? You build a sanctuary. In 2000, Animals Asia took over a run-down, twenty-five-acre animal facility in a beautifully lush bamboo forest, which the dedicated and dogged staff renovated and made ready to receive rescued bears.

To date, 40 bear farms have been closed and 247 bears have been rescued. Although the bears usually arrive in groups, each bear is rescued one at a time. Each is valuable, unique, and precious.

As each bear arrives at the sanctuary, she is assessed for catheters, medieval full-metal body jackets designed to keep her immobile, cage bars that have grown into her body, missing limbs cut off by unforgiving leg-hold traps when she was snared in the wild as a cub, claws that have curled and grown into her paw pads, and an unending list of other injustices. She then receives life-giving surgery and convalesces in a larger cage, where she can sit up and move around a bit. She is given physiotherapy to help develop muscles that have been critically immobile, and simple enrichment tasks such as reaching for her own food through the mesh ceiling of the cage. The new cage, although mercifully larger than the crate she was used to, is too small for permanent bear living, but it is a necessary step to help her to slowly acclimate, mentally and physically, to environments of greater and greater complexity. Once the wounds have healed, the bear is moved to a bedroom abutting the natural enclosure, where she will be introduced to other bears and heavily enriched several times a day.

In January 2006, the European Union voted unanimously to ask China to escalate the closing of bear bile farms and turn the bears over to Animals Asia. Embarrassed, the Chinese government responded by saying that it would continue with bear bile farming until a substitute could be found—something that has already been done in both traditional and Western medicine. The government also claimed that current bile-extraction techniques are painless, which is clearly nonsense, and that the opponents of bear bile farming are using old film footage, because things are much better now (the footage used by Animals Asia was less than a year old).[23] The organization is still receiving bears to meet the quota of five hundred animals from the agreement made in 2000. At the moment, it is unclear if Animals Asia will receive another five hundred bears. Animals Asia recognizes that the Chinese government has been a positive and willing partner in eradicating bear farms and that without their support there would not be a sanctuary or a program. What they and the European Union are suggesting is that it's time to push the baby buggy farther down the road and finish the stroll.

Animals Asia is busy rescuing bears in Vietnam, as well. In 2005, the Vietnamese government signed an agreement with Animals Asia to rescue two hundred bears from Vietnam's formerly thriving but now outlawed bear bile farming industry, which is estimated to warehouse about three thousand bears. Remarkably, Animals Asia has built another sanctuary, this one nestled in the lush forests bordering the Tam Dao National Park.

Understanding that deeply rooted change in societal mores lies with the next generation, Animals Asia staff and volunteers have presented thousands of programs for children of all ages, teaching them that bears, and all animals, are sentient beings deserving of our respect and compassion. They tackle the tough issues, such as the age-old practice of eating dogs and cats, who suffer immensely before they die. One particularly innovative program is called Dr. Dog, where volunteers take their pet dogs to patients in hospitals, the elderly in nursing homes, and children in schools. The dog ambassadors can always be counted on to play along by simply being themselves. Robinson's pragmatic belief is that empathy for one animal grows into empathy for many. It's a hugely successful program that is mushrooming throughout China and has helped to bring social standing and value to dogs as well as to fuel the new (to China) pet craze, which will, in turn, eventually prevent people from viewing companion animals as food items.

Animals Asia has done this work with the help of thousands of people around the world. There are many wonderful ways to get involved, all described on their Web site at www.animalsasia. org. You can sponsor individual bears at the sanctuaries, write letters to the Chinese government, or organize an information table at your local grocery store, library, church, or school to provide educational materials and ask folks to sign a petition and make donations. Check the Web site to see if there is a local Animals Asia support chapter near you and join their efforts; if there isn't, start a chapter in your community. Animals Asia offers two downloadable booklets, for children in grades one to three and grade four and up, with puzzles, information, and games.

Teachers can access teaching materials and ideas for classroom and schoolwide campaigns. Or you can shop at their gift shop online, where you can buy stuff for the bears at the sanctuaries and stuff for yourself. You can even purchase a limited edition print, by internationally acclaimed artist David Shepherd, of Jasper the Asiatic Black Bear.

Jill Robinson, who does this work because it is the right thing to do, has been given the honor of Member of the British Empire by Queen Elizabeth II and has had notables such as Jane Goodall, Olivia Newton-John, Australian celebrity veterinarian Katrina Warren, and Hong Kong superstar Karen Mok support the cause. Despite all of this, what seems to amaze Robinson more than any other thing in her incredible life is that the bears seem to forgive humans and allow the staff at the sanctuaries to care for them.

WHAT I HAVE found most rewarding in helping bears is that it is so effective: it truly makes a difference. Each bear rescued is fully cognizant that things are better now and takes full advantage of that fact. Sometimes in my work, a bear has looked back at me before moving on to the next thing and sometimes not; either way, the difference has registered.

You have already begun your bear work. Some of the proceeds from the sale of this book are donated to each organization mentioned in it. Take it one step farther and join me and thousands of others by getting involved. Whether you give your local bear rehabilitator a call, join your children in signing up for a program, contact an organization making a global difference, or simply tell a friend about polar bears, American black bear sanctuaries, or bear bile farms; if you do any of these things, you are making a difference to save a bear.

NOTES

CHAPTER 1

1 Jonathan Balcombe, *Pleasurable Kingdom: Animals and the Nature of Feeling Good* (New York: Macmillan, 1999), http://www.pleasurablekingdom.com (accessed November 27, 2008).

2 Stephen R. Kellert, *Kinship to Mastery: Biophilia in Human Evolution and Development* (Washington, D.C.: Island Press, 1997).

3 Gordon M. Burghardt, "Critical Anthropomorphism, Uncritical Anthropocentrism, and Naïve Nominalism," *Comparative Cognition & Behavior Reviews* 2 (2007): 136–38, http://psyc.queensu.ca/ccbr/ (accessed November 28, 2008).

4 Marc Bekoff, "Animal Emotions: Exploring Passionate Natures," *Bioscience* 50 (2000): 861–70.

5 S.C. Minta, K.A. Minta, and D.F. Lott, "Hunting Associations between Badgers (*Taxidea taxus*) and Coyotes (*Canis latrans*)," *Journal of Mammology* 73 (1992): 814–20.

6 Cindy Engel, *Wild Health: How Animals Keep Themselves Well and What We Can Learn From Them* (New York: Houghton Mifflin Company, 2002).

CHAPTER 2

1 Stephen Herrero, *Bear Attacks: Their Causes and Avoidance*, revised
   Canadian edition (Toronto: McClelland & Stewart Ltd., 2003).
2 *Ibid.*
3 Stephen Herrero, ed., *Biology, Demography, Ecology and Management
   of Grizzly Bears in and around Banff National Park and Kananaskis Country:
   The Final Report of the Eastern Slopes Grizzly Bear Project.* (Alberta:
   University of Calgary, 2005), http://www.canadianrockies.net/grizzly
   (accessed February 28, 2008).
4 *Ibid.*
5 Michael F. Proctor et al., "Gender-specific Dispersal Distances of Grizzly
   Bears Estimated by Genetic Analysis," *Canadian Journal of Zoology* 82
   (2004): 1108–18.
6 F.L. Bunnell and R.K. McCann, "The brown or grizzly bear" in Ian
   Sterling, ed., *Bears: Majestic Creatures of the Wild.* (Sydney: Weldon Owen
   Publishing, 1993): 88–95.
7 Stephen Herrero, *Grizzly Bears.*
8 Stephen Herrero, *Grizzly Bears.*

CHAPTER 3

1 Stephen Herrero and David Hamer, "Courtship and Copulation of a
   Pair of Grizzly Bears, with Comments on Reproductive Plasticity and
   Strategy," *Journal of Mammology* 58 (1977): 441–44.
2 *Ibid.*
3 William R. Boone et al., "Evidence that Bears Are Induced Ovulators,"
   Theriogenology 61 (2004): 1163–69.
4 Eva Bellemain et al., "The Dilemma of Female Mate Selection
   in the Brown Bear, a Species with Sexually Selected Infanticide,"
   Proceedings of the Royal Society, Biological Sciences 273 (2006):
   283–91.
5 Cindy Engel, *Wild Health.*
6 Bernd Heinrich, *Winter World: The Ingenuity of Animal Survival*
   (New York: Ecco, 2000).

CHAPTER 4

1 Ian Stirling, *Polar Bears* (Ann Arbor, MI: University of Michigan Press, 1998).
2 *Ibid.*
3 IUCN Species Survival Commission Polar Bear Specialist Group, http://pbsg.npolar.no/ (accessed November 28, 2008).
4 Jane Goodall, *In the Shadow of Man*, revised edition (Boston: Houghton Mifflin, 1988).
5 Dian Fossey, *Gorillas in the Mist* (Boston: Houghton Mifflin, Mariner Books, 2000).
6 Ian Stirling, *Polar Bears.*
7 Heini Hediger, *Wild Animals in Captivity* (London: Buttersworth Scientific Publications, 1950).
8 Donald J. Furnell and David Oolooyuk, "Polar Bear Predation of Ringed Seals in Ice-free Water," *Canadian Field Naturalist* 94 (1980): 88–89.
9 S.N. Atkinson and M.A. Ramsay, "The Effects of Prolonged Fasting on the Body Composition and Reproductive Success of Female Polar Bears (*Ursus maritimus*)," *Functional Ecology* 9 (1995): 559–67.
10 Andrew E. Derocher et al., "Terrestrial Foraging by Polar Bears during the Ice-free Period in Western Hudson Bay," *Arctic* 46 (1995): 251–54.

CHAPTER 5

1 Else M.B. Poulsen et al., "Use of Fluoxetine for the Treatment of Stereotypical Pacing Behavior in a Captive Polar Bear," *Journal of the American Veterinary Medical Association* 209 (1996): 1470–74.
2 Judith L. Rapoport, "The Biology of Obsessions and Compulsions," *Scientific American* 260 (1989): 82–89.
3 *Ibid.*
4 Else M.B. Poulsen, "Polar Bear Enrichment at the Calgary Zoo," *The Shape of Enrichment* 1 (1992): 10.
5 Ian Stirling, *Polar Bears.*
6 G. Mason and J. Rushen, *Stereotypic Animal Behaviour: Fundamentals and Applications to Welfare* (Wallingford-Oxon, U.K.: CABI, 2006).
7 Else Poulsen, "Fluoxetine."

8 Judith L. Rapoport, "Recent Advances in Obsessive-Compulsive Disorder," *Neuropsychopharmacology* 5 (1991): 1–10.
9 Judith L. Rapoport, *Biology of Obsessions and Compulsions*.
10 *Ibid.*
11 Else Poulsen, "Fluoxetine."
12 Ian Stirling, *Polar Bears*.
13 Else Poulsen, "Fluoxetine."

CHAPTER 6

1 Norbert Rosing, *The World of the Polar Bear* (Richmond Hill, ON: Firefly Books Ltd., 2006).

CHAPTER 7

1 Bernard Peyton, "Bear in the Eyebrow of the Jungle," *Animal Kingdom* 90 (1987): 38–45.
2 *Ibid.*
3 S. Paisley and D.L. Garshelis, "Activity Patterns and Time Budgets of Andean Bears (*Tremarctos ornatus*) in the Apolobamba Range of Bolivia," *Journal of Zoology* 268 (2006): 25–34.
4 IUCN, 2008 Red List of Threatened Species, http://www.iucnredlist.org (accessed November 28, 2008).
5 *Ibid.*
6 R.R. Peel, J. Price, and P. Karsten, "Mother-rearing of a Spectacled Bear Cub *Tremarctos ornatus* at Calgary Zoo," *International Zoo Yearbook* 19 (1979): 177–85.
7 David Morales, "Queens Zoo Andean Bear Program: A Diverse and Expanding Captive Management Program," *Bear Information Exchange for Rehabilitators, Zoos and Sanctuaries 2007 Proceedings Abstract*, 2007.
8 Glenda Misurelli, "Activity Patterns and Behaviors of Captive Spectacled Bears (*Tremarctos ornatus*)" (Calgary Zoo Apprenticeship Program Submission, 1991).
9 Terry D. Debruyn, *Walking with Bears: One Man's Relationship with Three Generations of Wild Bears* (New York: Lyons Press, 1999).

10 Else Poulsen and Elaine Willms, "Eradicating Baldness and Pacing in Two Captive Andean Bears," *Animal Keepers' Forum* 28 (2001): 165–72.

11 Karen Pryor, *Don't Shoot the Dog: The New Art of Teaching and Training*, revised edition (New York: Bantam Books, 1999).

12 Elaine Willms, "Baseline Behaviours of a Female Spectacled Bear (*Tremarctos ornatus*)" (Calgary Zoo Apprenticeship Program Submission, 2000).

13 Else Poulsen and Elaine Willms, "Eradicating Baldness and Pacing."

CHAPTER 8

1 L.L. Rogers, "Aiding the Wild Survival of Orphaned Bear Cubs," *Wildlife Rehabilitation* 4 (1985): 104–11.

2 Sally Maughn, "Handbook" (Garden City, ID: Idaho Black Bear Rehab, Inc., 2004), http://www.bearrehab.org/2008completehandbook.pdf (accessed November 28, 2008).

3 John Beecham, "Orphan Bear Cubs: Rehabilitation and Release Guidelines" (Toronto: World Society for the Protection of Animals, 2006), http://www.bearsmart.com/managingBears/JB_Rehab_report.pdf (accessed November 28, 2008).

4 Terry D. DeBruyn, *Walking with Bears*.

5 B. Kilham and E. Gray, *Among the Bears: Raising Orphan Cubs in the Wild* (New York: Henry Holt, 2002).

6 John Beecham, "Orphan Bear Cubs."

7 B. Kilham and E. Gray, *Among the Bears*.

CHAPTER 9

1 Bruce Owen, "Polar Bears in Mexico Circus; Province of Manitoba, Activists Appalled," *Winnipeg Free Press*, March 29, 1996.

2 Bruce Owen, "Crusade Seeks End to Polar Bear Trade," *Winnipeg Free Press*, March 29, 1996.

3 *The Polar Bear Protection Act*, S.M. 2002, c. 25.

4 Polar Bears Alive, "Polar bears home for the holidays" (Baton Rouge, LA: Polar Bears International, 2002), http://www.polarbearsalive.org/circusbears.htm (accessed November 28, 2008).

5 People for the Ethical Treatment of Animals (PETA), video clip of polar bears languishing in filthy cages in the sweltering heat of Puerto Rico at the Suarez Brothers Circus, http://www.petatv.com/tvpopup/video.asp?video=suarez_polar (accessed November 28, 2008).

6 People for the Ethical Treatment of Animals (PETA), photos of polar bears sweltering in the tropical heat, http://www.circuses.com/polarphotos.asp (accessed November 28, 2008).

CHAPTER 10

1 Detroit Zoo, series of videos from November 22, 2004 to September 2005 of Bärle raising Talini, her cub, http://www.detroitzoo.org/Animals/Animals/Online_Movies (accessed November 28, 2008).

EPILOGUE

1 2008 IUCN Red List of Threatened Species, http://www.iucnredlist.org/search (accessed October 25, 2008).

2 *Ibid.*

3 *Ibid.*

4 Harry Reynolds, "Gobi bears," *International Bear News*, 14.1 (2005): 3, http://www.bearbiology.com/iba/ibno1.html (accessed November 28, 2008).

5 Darcy Henton, "Gov't to launch grizzly bear recovery plan," *Edmonton Journal*, October 5, 2007. http://www.canada.com/edmontonjournal/news/story.html?id=82fb947d-eefe-45ac-a228-f8b71795450a&k=5597 (accessed November 28, 2008).

6 Environment Canada, Species at Risk List, http://www.sararegistry.gc.ca (accessed November 28, 2008).

7 ESCC Scientific Sub-committee, "Status Evaluation for the Grizzly Bear (*Ursus arctos*) in Alberta" (Edmonton: Alberta Endangered Species Conservation Committee, 2002: p 3, http://www.srd.gov.ab.ca/fishwildlife/escc/speciesassessed.aspx (accessed November 28, 2008).

8 Paraphrased from Indy's ex-girlfriend Marion Ravenwood, who comments "Yeah, everybody's sorry. Abner was sorry for draggin' me all over this earth lookin' for his little bits of [archaeological] junk. I'm

sorry to still be stuck in this dive. Everybody's sorry for something," in the 1981 Steven Spielberg movie *Indiana Jones: Raiders of the Lost Ark.*

9   Ian Stirling, "How Bears Came to Be" in *Bears: Majestic Creatures of the Wild* (New York: Rodale Press, 1993). Today's spectacled bear is the only living decendant of the giant short-faced bear, the biggest bear ever to have lived, which was indigenous to southern North America some ten thousand years ago.

10 R.D. Appleton et al., "Mark-resight Population Estimates Derived from Observations of Andean Bears Using Water-holes in the Tropical Dry Forests of Peru," *The 18th International Conference on Bear Research and Management Proceedings* (International Association for Bear Research and Management, 2007).

11 *Ibid.*

12 Gail Hedberg, "Hand-rearing polar bears" in Laurie Gage, ed., *Hand-rearing of Wild and Domestic Mammals* (Ames, ID: Iowa State Press, 2002).

13 Gail Hedberg et al., "Pathogenesis of Metabolic Bone Disease in Captive Polar Bears (*Ursus maritimus*)," in *International Polar Bear Husbandry Conference Proceedings* (Sebastopol, CA: Polar Bears International, February 4–7, 2004), http://www.polarbearsinternational.org/ipbhc/nutrition/presentations (accessed November 28, 2008).

14 G.E. Hedberg, et al., "Speculations on Pathogenesis of Metabolic Bone Disease in Captive Polar Bears (*Ursus maritimus*) with Links to Taurine Status" in *5th European Zoo Nutrition Conference* (Chester, U.K., January 24–27, 2008).

15 Canadian Federation of Humane Societies, "Senate allows bear cub abuser to escape animal cruelty charge," *The Voice for Animal Welfare*, September 11, 2003.

16 International Fund for Animal Welfare (IFAW), "Help stop animal cruelty in Canada," 2008.

17 International Fund for Animal Welfare (IFAW), "Buddy bear back in the wild," 2004.

18 The Aspen Valley Wildlife Sanctuary (AVWS), "Aspen Valley Recipient of IFAW 2004 Animal Action Award!," 2004, http://www.aspenvalley wildlifesanctuary.com/news_action.html (accessed November 28, 2008).

19 Convention on International Trade in Endangered Species (CITES) Appendices I to III, 2008, http://www.cites.org/eng/app/appendices.shtml (accessed November 28, 2008).

20 S. Akare et al., "Ursodeoxycholic Acid Modulates Histone Acetylation and Induces Differentiation and Senescence," *International Journal of Cancer* 119 (2006): 2958–69.

21 Interpol, "Operation bear net," 2008, http://www.interpol.int/public/ EnvironmentalCrime/Wildlife/SuccessStories20070531.asp#bearnet (accessed February 28, 2008).

22 Donald N. Blakeley, "Listening to the Animals: The Confucian View of Animal Welfare," *Journal of Chinese Philosophy* 30 (2003): 137–57.

23 Jane Macartney, "Siphoning Bear Bile for Medicine Is Painless, Says China," *The Times*, January 13, 2006, http://www.timesonline.co.uk/tol/news/ world/asia/article1081920.ece (accessed February 28, 2008).

APPENDIX

ANIMALS ASIA
Jill Robinson, Founder

An organization dedicated to ending cruelty and restoring respect for animals in Asia, particularly focusing on the rehabilitation of Asian black bears rescued from the bear bile farming industry in China and Vietnam.

> Hong Kong Head Office
> 2/F, Room 04–05, Nam Wo Hong Building
> 148 Wing Lok Street
> Sheung Wan, Hong Kong

> Hong Kong Post Box
> P.O. Box 374 General Post Office Hong Kong
> Tel: +852-2791-2225 Fax: +852-2791-2320
> e-mail: info@animalsasia.org
> Web site: www.animalsasia.org

ASPEN VALLEY WILDLIFE SANCTUARY
Audrey Tourney, Founder

The world's largest bear rehabilitation facility, dedicated to wildlife rescue, rehabilitation, and release.

> Aspen Valley Wildlife Sanctuary
> 1116 Crawford Street
> Rosseau, Ontario POC 1J0
> Canada
> Tel: 705-732-6368 Fax: 705-732-1929
> e-mail: aspen@vianet.on.ca
> Web site: www.aspenvalleywildlifesanctuary.com

ASSOCIATION OF ZOOS AND AQUARIUMS (AZA)

An organization that can help you find your local accredited zoo and get involved in their bear conservation programs.

> 8403 Colesville Road, Suite 710
> Silver Spring, Maryland 20910
> USA
> Tel: 301-562-0777 Fax: 301-562-0888
> Web site: www.aza.org

BEAR CARE GROUP (BCG)
Else Poulsen and Gail Hedberg, Founders

This group facilitates professional collaboration between bear care professionals in zoos, sanctuaries, and rehabilitation facilities through venues such as conferences to promote bear care excellence.

> P.O. Box 4394
> Troy, Michigan 48099
> USA
> e-mail: info@bearcaregroup.org
> Web site: www.bearcaregroup.org

CANADIAN ASSOCIATION OF ZOOS AND AQUARIUMS (CAZA)

An organization that can help you find your local Canadian accredited zoo and get involved in their bear conservation programs.

>280 Metcalfe Street, Suite 400
>Ottawa, Ontario K2P IR7
>Canada
>Tel: 613-567-0099 or 1-888-822-2907 Fax: 613-233-5438
>e-mail: info@caza.ca
>Web site: www.caza.ca

DESERT ANDEAN BEAR RESEARCH PROJECT—PERU
Robyn Appleton, Bear Biologist

A research project to identify where and how the newly discovered desert Andean bears live and how we can conserve them and their habitat.

>P.O. Box 5209
>Squamish, British Columbia V8B 0C2
>Canada
>email: Robyn@spectacledbearconservation.com
>Web site: http://spectacledbearconservation.com/index.html

FOUR PAWS

An organization that advocates for and champions the welfare of abused animals. Activities include the rescue, rehabilitation, and release of bears into natural habitat sanctuaries.

>32–36 Loman Street
>London SEI OEE
>UK
>Tel: +0207-922-7954
>Web site: www.fourpaws.org.uk

IDAHO BLACK BEAR REHAB
Sally Maughn, Founder

A rehabilitation facility dedicated exclusively to the rescue and rehabilitation of American black bears.

> 6097 Arney Lane
> Garden City, Idaho 83714
> USA
> e-mail: info@bearrehab.org
> Web site: www.bearrehab.org

INTERNATIONAL ASSOCIATION FOR BEAR RESEARCH AND MANAGEMENT (IBA)
Karen Noyce, Chair

The association of bear researchers and professionals. Their Bear Conservation Fund, accessible on their Web site, allows everyone to participate in supporting wild bear research and conservation projects around the world. The fund was launched to propel vital programs forward in the face of accelerating threats to bear populations.

> 115542 County Road 72
> Warba, Minnesota 55793
> USA
> Tel: 218-259-6686
> e-mail: karen_noyce@bearbiology.com
> Web site: www.bearbiology.com

INTERNATIONAL FUND FOR ANIMAL WELFARE (IFAW)

The fund seeks to improve the welfare of wild and domestic animals by reducing commercial exploitation of animals, protecting wildlife habitats, and helping animals in distress. They are active in Asia, working to help bears in the bear bile farming industry.

290 Summer Street
Yarmouth Port, Maine 02675
USA
Tel: 508-744-2000 or 1-800-932-4329 Fax: 508-744-2009
e-mail: info@ifaw.org
Web site: www.ifaw.org

NATIONAL WILDLIFE REHABILITATORS ASSOCIATION (NWRA)

An organization that can help you find a bear rehabilitator near you in
North America.

2625 Clearwater Road, Suite 110
St. Cloud, Minnesota 56301
USA
Tel: 320-230-9920 Fax: 320-230-3077
e-mail: NWRA@nwrawildlife.org
Web site: www.nwrawildlife.org

PEACE RIVER REFUGE & RANCH

An American sanctuary housing numerous bears as well as other species.

P.O. Box 1127
2545 Stoner Lane
Zolfo Springs, Florida 33890
USA
Tel: 863-735-0804 Fax: 863-735-0805
e-mail: info@peaceriverrefuge.org
Web site: www.peaceriverrefuge.org

POLAR BEARS INTERNATIONAL (PBI)
Robert W. Buchanan, President

PBI is an organization dedicated exclusively to polar bear conservation,
spearheading global polar bear conservation education programs and
supporting wild and captive polar bear research that benefits bears directly.

> PBI
> 105 Morris Street, Suite 188
> Sebastopol, California 95472
> USA
>
> PBI–Canada
> 5 Donald Street, Suite 550
> Winnipeg, Manitoba R3L 2T4
> Canada
> Web site: www.polarbearsinternational.org

THE ASSOCIATION OF SANCTUARIES (TAOS)

An organization that can help you find an accredited bear sanctuary in
North America.

> P.O. Box 925
> Stillwater, Minnesota 55082
> USA
> Tel: 763-772-3087 Fax: 651-275-0457
> e-mail: info@taosanctuaries.org
> Web site: http://www.taosanctuaries.org

WILDLIFE SOS

Dedicated to the preservation and protection of wildlife and their
environment, the group rescues and rehabilitates sloth bears abused as
India's dancing bears and runs three bear sanctuaries.

406 East 300, Suite 302
Salt Lake City, Utah 84111
USA
e-mail: info@wildlifesosusa.org
Web site www.wildlifesos.org

WORLD SOCIETY FOR THE PROTECTION OF ANIMALS (WSPA)

An animal welfare organization assisting animals in need around the world. Its activities include the rescue and rehabilitation of bears, some of which can be released back into the wild, while others are released into natural habitat sanctuaries.

Lincoln Plaza
89 South Street, Suite 201
Boston, Maine 02111
USA
Tel: 1-800-883-9772 Fax: 617-737-4404
Web site: www.wspa-usa.org